FOR OFFICIAL USE ONLY.

SUMMARY OF MACHINE GUN INTELLIGENCE

No. 1
No. 2
No. 3

Issued by General Staff, War Office.

MAY, JUNE, JULY, 1917

THE MACHINE GUN SCHOOL,
MACHINE GUN TRAINING CENTRE

The Naval & Military Press Ltd

Published by the
The Naval & Military Press
in association with the Royal Armouries

Unit 10 Ridgewood Industrial Park,
Uckfield, East Sussex, TN22 5QE
Tel: +44 (0) 1825 749494
Fax: +44 (0) 1825 765701

MILITARY HISTORY AT YOUR FINGERTIPS
www.naval-military-press.com

ONLINE GENEALOGY RESEARCH
www.military-genealogy.com

ONLINE MILITARY CARTOGRAPHY
www.militarymaproom.com

The Library & Archives Department at the Royal Armouries Museum, Leeds, specialises in the history and development of armour and weapons from earliest times to the present day. Material relating to the development of artillery and modern fortifications is held at the Royal Armouries Museum, Fort Nelson.

For further information contact:
Royal Armouries Museum, Library, Armouries Drive,
Leeds, West Yorkshire LS10 1LT
Royal Armouries, Library, Fort Nelson, Down End Road, Fareham PO17 6AN

Or visit the Museum's website at
www.armouries.org.uk

In reprinting in facsimile from the original, any imperfections are inevitably reproduced and the quality may fall short of modern type and cartographic standards.

CONFIDENTIAL.

$\frac{121}{\text{FRANCE}}$
608

FOR OFFICIAL USE ONLY.

SUMMARY OF MACHINE GUN INTELLIGENCE

No. 1.

Issued by General Staff, War Office.

MAY, 1917.

PRINTED AT THE MACHINE GUN SCHOOL, MACHINE GUN TRAINING CENTRE.
UNDER THE AUTHORITY OF HIS MAJESTY'S STATIONERY OFFICE,

CONTENTS.

Part I. Training.

Section *a*. Personnel.
,, *b*. Transport.
,, *c*. Co-operation.
,, *d*. Gas.
,, *e*. Operations—Notes on.
,, *f*. General.

Part II. Technical.

Section *a*. Equipment.
,, *b*. Demonstrations.
,, *c*. Experiments.
,, *d*. Tests.
,, *e*. General.

Part III.
Machine Gun Intelligence of Foreign Countries.

Section *a*. Tactics.
,, *b*. Equipment.
,, *c*. Organization.
,, *d*. General.

NOTE.—With the exception of those paragraphs marked with an asterisk, the information contained in this summary has been extracted from reports received from General Headquarters of Expeditionary Forces.

PART I.—TRAINING.

Section A.—PERSONNEL.

(1) TRAINING OF SCOUTS.

The necessity of training scouts in machine gun companies is pointed out. Special training is carried out at the M.G.T.C. for all Machine Gun Company scouts.

Section B.—TRANSPORT.

(2) Companies are receiving more instruction in the uses and fitting of pack saddlery, and mules should be trained to carry pack loads.

Improvised methods of carrying M.G. and Equipment are under consideration of the M.G.T.C. (see also para. 3).

The great value of pack transport was brought out in the offensive in April.

Ammunition was carried in many cases right up to the forward guns.

Pack animals must be used boldly, and the transport should remain under the control of the Company Commander and not left with B echelon.

(3) PACK SADDLES (Notes by a Machine Gun Company).

We have practised carrying our guns and kit on pack animals, and have found a satisfactory method of carrying guns and tripods on pack saddles by fixing them with the aid of stirrup leathers. For the gun, the leather is passed about twice round the middle of the leather gun case, and strapped. A small strap is also passed round this case and through the rear arch of the saddle.

The tripod is fixed similarly by passing the stirrup leather twice round the junction of the legs, crosshead to the front and downwards. Care should be taken that the clamp rests on the pad of the saddle and not on the flap, or horse's back.

Ammunition may be carried in a similar manner by strapping four boxes together with the stirrup leather and loading them so that two boxes of each four are on either side of the saddle, making four boxes on each side of the horses.

Section C.—CO-OPERATION.

(4) WITH INFANTRY : ADVANCE OF MACHINE GUNS.

Vickers Guns pushed up in support of the infantry should be so disposed as to provide for the following :—
- (a) Overhead and covering fire for the next stage of the advance, wherever possible.
- (b) Protection to the flanks of the infantry during and after consolidation.
- (c) Forming supporting or rallying points for the infantry in case of retirement.
- (d) Dealing with enemy counter-attacks.

As a general rule the following dispositions on a Brigade front are recommended for the above purposes :—

1 section pushed up on the flanks with the infantry.

2 sections disposed to give covering fire, and to form supporting points.

1 section in reserve.

The new Syllabus of Training at the M.G.T.C. Schools is based on constant co-operation with infantry.

(5) WITH ARTILLERY.

During the present semi-open warfare, which necessitates artillery being boldly pushed forward and risking capture in case of hostile counter-attack, it is essential that machine guns should consolidate in depth so that if the leading infantry get rushed, artillery may still be protected. It is not sufficiently realised that machine gun fire from positions in rear or to the flanks is often the most effective. This and the necessity of reconnaissance must be firmly impressed upon all M.G. Section and Company Commanders. Field batteries in forward positions require local protection. This can best be given by machine guns placed well to the flanks of the gun positions, and under the orders of the F.A. Brigade Commander.

(6) WITH R.E.

When arranging for the consolidation of a "zone of resistance," the first essential is to select and fix the position of obstacles (*e.g.*, belts of wire), and machine guns, in conjunction with each other. The Divisional and Brigade Machine Gun Officer should accompany the G.S.O. and R.E. Officer when they go over the ground before any work is started, settle the sites of emplacements, and mark them on a map and also on the ground.

Section D.—GAS.

(7) A further case of poisoning by cordite fumes occurred in a covered emplacement.

In this case 1,000 rounds were fired in bursts of 10, the last two bursts being 40 rounds. No. 1 then fainted. Firing was stopped, and the Officer and No. 2, who were also in the emplacement, turned subsequently sick and faint. The weather was windy. A large number of rounds have since been fired from this emplacement by men wearing respirators without any ill-effects. Experiments are being conducted in a model emplacement, but have not yet been completed.

(8) FUMES IN M.G. EMPLACEMENTS.

With reference to the poisoning of gun crews in closed emplacements by carbon monoxide gas, experiments are being made by lighting a "Tommy's Cooker," with a suitable flue, in order to create a draught. The use of the ordinary anti-gas fan is not effective in dealing with the fumes.

Section E.—OPERATIONS, Notes on

(9) ORDERS TO MACHINE GUNS.

The failure to issue operation orders in sufficient time, or failing that, a warning order, has at times interfered with the proper employment of machine guns. A large amount of reconnaissance is necessary to get full value from these guns, and if ample time is not given, their effectiveness is sure to suffer.

(10) CONSOLIDATION.

There is great lack of forethought in consolidation, the guns being placed as a rule in trenches recently evacuated by the enemy, when they should have been placed in ground some yards in front or behind, possibly in shell holes (which should afford good fields of fire). The old trenches being accurately known by the enemy's artillery, little hope of keeping guns in action for any length of time in them can be entertained; one instance—a section of guns was destroyed by trench mortar fire and captured.

(11) CO-ORDINATION AFTER ATTACK.

It is suggested that, as soon as a defensive position is taken up to be occupied for any time, the O.C. Machine Gun Company should be at once informed, in order that he may co-ordinate the guns on the Brigade front and arrange for co-operation between his guns and also with the guns on the right and left of the Brigade front his Company is covering.

(12) BARRAGE FIRE.

Barrages of Vickers Guns gave excellent results when worked out carefully beforehand, but not much success was achieved by them in later stages of the operations, in cases where they had to be improvised.

Experience showed :—

- (a) That they should, where possible, be practised beforehand with the artillery barrages.
- (b) That plans for later barrages should be worked out beforehand as thoroughly as possible from the map and from observation of the ground to be taken. These plans should be very simple, and should be confined to the front of single brigades, in order to prevent dislocation by the failure of flank units.
- (c) That careful arrangements should be made beforehand for liaison between advanced guns and the M.G. Coy. Commander.
- (d) When a machine gun barrage is intended, it should be practised with the artillery barrage so that the enemy may be deceived as to the actual time of the attack.

(13) EFFECT OF BARRAGE FIRE.

(a) *Effect on Enemy.*—During the early stages of operations, which commenced on the 9th April, large numbers of the enemy were seen to drop in areas under machine gun fire where no shells were bursting. (The small number of enemy machine guns in action was possibly due to the systematic searching of the ground in the vicinity of emplacements destroyed by our artillery.)

Movements of the enemy from front to rear were on several occasions stopped, both before and after *zero*.

One German prisoner stated that it was impossible to leave dugouts in the village of Tilloy owing to the hail of bullets directed on this locality.

(b) *Barrage Fire during an Advance.*—Indirect overhead barrage fire was carried out prior to the attack upon LIERAMONT (8,000 rounds), HEUDICOURT (24,000 rounds), GAUCHE WOOD (45,000 rounds), VILLERS GUISLAIN (two days, 81,000 rounds) and GONNELIEU (17,000 rounds). There was no direct evidence of the destructive effect of this fire, but on every occasion on which it was brought to bear the objective was gained. No counter-attacks developed on that front.

(c) *Effect on our own Troops.*—During, and since the operations many reports have been received as to the efficiency of this fire. During the latter phases of the operations many barrages were asked for. No complaints whatever were received as regards the safety limits employed.

(14) Cavalry Machine Gun Tactics.

In the fighting in April, one section was attached to each regiment.

The Officers commanding regiments attached one sub-section to the leading squadrons.

Each of the advanced squadrons moved with one troop split up in patrols in front, three troops in line of troop columns and M. G. sub-section roughly in rear of these. This proved a satisfactory formation for going through heavy shell fire.

When advancing mounted under heavy fire there is a grave risk of guns being put out of action through the ammunition pack horses being killed or wounded or getting loose.

It is suggested that certain gun numbers should carry empty belts (on the men, not on the horse) as S.A.A. is very easily picked up or taken from bandoliers, an thus the gun would not be put absolutely out of action by the ammunition pack horses being hit or getting loose.

(15) Machine Guns in Advanced Guard Actions.

Action of a Machine Gun Company in the Attack on Francilly-Selency and Selency, 2nd April, 1917.—During the operations in the taking of the villages of Francilly-Selency and Selency on the 2nd April, 1917, one of the guns detailed to go forward with the infantry was handled with boldness. It was got quickly into action in Francilly-Selency as soon as the village was taken, and immediately opened fire on a party of the enemy, estimated at 500, who were seen in Selency. Fire was opened at a range of 800 yards. The fire of this gun was effective, and the enemy bolted. By this time two other guns, which the Section Commander had called up, were in action, and also fired on the retreating enemy, inflicting severe losses on them, with the result that the village of Selency was taken with little or no loss to ourselves. Many of the enemy were found dead in the village and vicinity who were killed by this fire.

During the same operations, a hostile 77 mm. battery in action about 800 yards S.E. of Francilly-Selency, was engaging our troops at 1,000 yards range with such effect that their position was becoming untenable. This was observed by a Machine Gun Officer, who pushed one of his guns slightly forward east of Francilly-Selency, engaged the hostile battery, and succeeded in silencing it and the gunners whenever they attempted to fire their guns. Our infantry were then able to dig in and consolidate their position. This latter machine gun was in action for two hours, and was eventually destroyed by a direct hit with a 15 cm. shell.

None of these guns had time to dig in, but took advantage of natural features in the ground for concealment.

LESSONS LEARNT.

    (i.) Initiative of Machine Gun Officer in appreciating the position and acting with boldness.

    (ii.) Deadly effect of machine gun fire against artillery in the open at close range.

    (iii.) Value of machine guns being well forward in advance guards.

(16) GENERAL.

The tactical employment of machine guns has greatly developed during the recent advance. The rapid improvement in the methods of handling guns has been remarkable. Officers, however, still require more initiative, in order to make opportunities for themselves rather than expect them to arise.

Early in the present operations it was the practice to allot machine guns liberally to Battalion Commanders, but latterly to a certain extent, owing to the difficulty of obtaining concealed approaches and the shorter advances made, the guns have been more frequently kept under the hands of the Brigade Commanders. In many instances all the guns have been detailed to their respective tasks by the Brigade Commander.

The general use of machine guns for covering the advance at long ranges necessitates the grouping of guns. The size of these groups tends to increase, to enable an area to be covered effectively.

When these large groups are carefully concealed, the surprise they have been able to bring on enemy positions has been such that the enemy has been pinned to his trenches, and his rifle defence against our attack has been small and occasionally nil.

There are instances where a second or part of a second Machine Gun Company has co-operated in an attack made by a brigade, with gratifying results. The additional sections, whatever the number, should be given a definite task, and not be placed under the command of the attacking Brigade M. G. Company Commander. A Company Commander cannot direct effectively more than four sections.

The large number of rounds expended by one Machine Gun Company makes the question of the supply of ammunition an important one. Company Commanders have had at times difficulty in supplying their guns. There is a decided tendency to keep the fighting limbered wagons too far back. The limbered wagons of a Machine Gun Company must not be looked upon as transport. They contain the first supply of ammunition for the guns, and other equipment necessary for the efficient fighting of the guns.

The enveloping tactics employed by the infantry, often, but by no means always, necessitate the employment of overhead or indirect fire, and sometimes both. These methods of fire have been employed with success. They are safe, provided that the Infantry and Machine Gun Commanders co-operate, and the intentions of both Commanders are clearly understood.

The need for Clinometers in open fighting is just as great as in trench warfare.

There have been practically no stoppages which might have been avoided in spite of much unfavourable weather. This is mainly due to the good instruction in mechanism given to the men before drafting, and the care taken of the gun in the field.

Range-finders have been proved to be essential for semi-open warfare.

Section F.—GENERAL.

(17) EXTRACT FROM "ORGANIZATION OF AN INFANTRY BATTALION."*

The essence of this (Platoon) organization is :—

That one Lewis Gun with its detachment is allotted to each platoon. Although this will be the normal organization, it may often be advisable in dealing with particular tactical situations to allot a second Lewis Gun to a platoon, or to withdraw temporarily one, two, or more of these guns from platoons for special tactical employment under the orders of the Company or Battalion Commanders. It is to be understood clearly that the normal organization is not to interfere with any such temporary special grouping or employment as circumstances may render desirable.

(18) ADVANCE OF M.G. SECTIONS.

In a gradual advance, when forward sections are in a strong position, it was found best to move the rear sections through the advanced sections on to a new line, the original advanced sections becoming the second line of defence.

PART II.—TECHNICAL.

Section A.—EQUIPMENT.

(19) DEPRESSION STOPS.*

The "Tate" pattern of depression stop is now in the hands of the Ministry of Munitions.

(20) TRAVERSING STOPS.*

A design has been submitted to the Ministry of Munitions in the form of two small stops which can be clamped in any position on to the traversing dial.

(21) DIRECTION DIAL.*

A new pattern is being made by Ministry of Munitions in which the dial itself is rotatable, and can be set to read Zero when the gun is pointing in any desired direction. It is graduated 0 to 180° in both directions.

(22) "ANDERSON" INDIRECT FIRE ATTACHMENT.

This attachment allows of fire being applied laterally over a distance of 3,000 yards (1,500 yards each side of Zero line) and vertically between two points 1,400 yards apart. The principle on which it works is that the trace of the trench line, track, etc., to be swept is plotted on to a curved record board attached to the traversing handles of the gun (which is pivotted to the tripod of the gun at one pivot only) works in the slot cut out and thus automatically follows the trace of the trench. The record boards are inter-changeable and can be prepared for any special target, within their limits, in half an hour after the gun position has been selected. This has been employed in one Corps, and details are circulated for information.

(23) CONDENSER TUBE ATTACHMENT.*

A new pattern is being introduced. The tube is connected to the gun by means of a brass angle piece, thus avoiding constant bending and damage at this point. This is in the hands of the Ministry of Munitions.

(24) BELT BOXES.

A suggestion has been made that a form of box similar to the German pattern, but to hold only one belt, would be preferable to the present types of wooden or metal boxes. Opinions are requested upon this.

(25) FLASH ABSORBER.*

For Vickers Gun, on same lines as used on some German Guns is in hands of Ministry of Munitions. Tests at M.G.T.C. proved quite successful.

(26) S.A.A.

It is suggested that S.A.A. for Machine Guns and Lewis Guns should be supplied in packets of cheap cotton belts packed in air-tight boxes. This would be much simpler and save time in filling belts and drums and save expenditure of clips. The average expenditure of S.A.A. is greater with Machine Guns and Lewis Guns than with rifles.

Section B.—DEMONSTRATIONS.

(27) BARRAGE FIRE (INDIRECT).*

A demonstration was fired on the 12th March, 1917, at the M.G.T.C., with a view to testing the statement contained in forthcoming "Notes and Rules for Barrage Fire for Machine Guns," that somewhere about 50 per cent. casualties may be expected in a hostile force moving through a barrage where the frontage covered by each gun is equal to four times the gradient of the descent of the bullet at the range used.

Particulars of the test :—

```
Range         = 1750.
Number of Guns = 4.
Gradient      = 1 in 8·5.
Front per Gun = 36 yards.
Total Front   = 144 yards.
```

The area fired at was a rectangle having sides about 144 yards.

The area was covered uniformly by 274 screens, each 10 ft. by 3 ft.

Depth of 90 per cent. B. Z. = 145 yards.

Time necessary to pass over this distance at $2\frac{1}{2}$ miles per hour (73 yards per minute) = 2 minutes.

Rounds per gun = 2 × 300 = 600.

Guns were registered on the flanks of the area before firing the test, and were fired as follows :—

Nos. 1 and 4 guns laid on flanks and traversed inwards.
,,   2 ,, 3 ,,   ,, centre ,,   ,, outwards.

Each gun (if fire had been continuous) would have traversed continuously between the flank limits.

Each screen was divided by vertical lines into rectangles 20 inches wide, giving 1,644 spaces in all.

Two tests were fired:

1. Hits on Screens = 623
   Spaces hit = 455 = 27·7 per cent. of total spaces.
2. Hits on Screens = 570
   Spaces hit = 441 = 26·8 per cent. of total spaces.

Owing to lack of screens only 41 per cent. of the rounds fired could possibly have hit the screens.

Owing to poor registration, due to difficulty of observation, some of the fire fell slightly outside the area screened. This, of course, would be of little importance in practice, as the enemy must pass through it.

Calculations, based on the known laws of probability, show that these results confirm the statement that about 50 per cent. casualties may be expected from a barrage of this description.

A second demonstration was fired on the 17th April, 1917, under approximately the same conditions.

> The area engaged was 140 yards by 140 yards.
> The number of screens was 260.
> 3450 rounds were fired from 4 guns in 3 minutes 16 seconds.
> 211 of the 260 screens were hit, and the total of hits registered was 717.

The above results were therefore again confirmed.

(28) BAND OF FIRE.*

METHOD OF ARRANGEMENT.—24 running figures, on small 4-wheel trucks, extended to four paces, pass through a Machine Gun Band of Fire, when the trucks are travelling at about 4 miles an hour.

The band of fire strikes the figures nearly in enfilade but the figures are so arranged that no shot can strike two figures.

RESULT.

(i.) Approximate rate of fire, 400 rounds per minute.
(ii.) Approximate time taken for line to pass through belt, 12 secs.
(iii.) Approximate number of rounds fired while figures pass through the belt, 80.
(iv.) Range to target, 400 to 475.
(v.) Sighting elevation, 500 yards.
(vi.) 33 Effectual hits on 20 figures. 3 Hits on rifle and pack.
(vii.) Percentage of casualties to force engaged, 83·3.

REMARKS.

A demonstration of this nature shows the importance of :—
(a) Selecting a position from which the fire power of the gun is at a maximum, viz., from an enfilade or nearly enfilade position.

(b) Selection of ground so that the dangerous zone is at a maximum (on level ground about 600 yards would probably be the limit).
(c) Careful selection of the aiming mark and alignment of gun before the target appears. The aiming mark should be near to the gun so that there is no possibility of it being masked by intervening troops.
(d) Accuracy of range and sighting of the gun.
(e) Taking every possible precaution against a stoppage in the gun.
(f) Maintaining the highest rate of fire with no pauses during the period the enemy are passing through the band.

REMARKS ON DEMONSTRATION FIRED.

One missfire occurred. This delayed the firer about 3 seconds and enabled 3 figures to get through the band.

A grand total of 36 hits on the complete figures out of an approximate 80 rounds which might have struck the figure shows that 45 per cent. of the 80 rounds hit the complete figures.

Section C.—EXPERIMENTS.

(29) COMPASS TOWER.*

The "Compass Tower," shown in the illustration, has been designed for the purpose of laying the gun accurately and quickly on any given bearing by direct use of the compass.

Experiments showed that the iron of the tripod did not affect the readings of a compass placed directly above the socket at a height of not less than 14 inches (the gun having been removed).

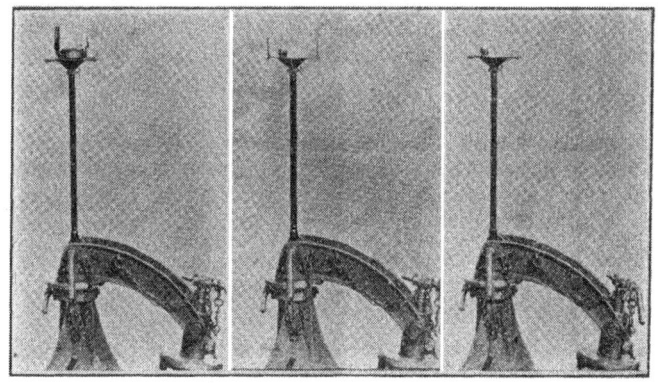

From the photograph it will be seen that the tower, made of a non-magnetic metal, is constructed so that it is held upright by the crosshead joint pin. On the table forming the top of the instrument is clamped a compass. The crosshead joint pin makes an angle of 90 with the bore of the gun, and the compass can be adjusted rapidly, by means of two small sight vanes, so that the lubber line is at right angles to the crosshead joint pin, *i.e.*, parallel to the bore of the gun. The sight vanes, when not in use, fold away under the table. The table is easily removable, and can be carried in the pocket; the stalk can be carried in a pack or haversack. Weight, $1\frac{1}{2}$ lbs.; length, 16 inches; made of gun-metal.

The method of use is as follows :—

To lay the gun on any known magnetic bearing, remove the gun from the crosshead to a distance of at least 5 yards. Place the tower in position on the crosshead, securing it by means of the crosshead joint pin. Loosen the traversing clamp, and turn the crosshead until the required reading is seen on looking through the compass prism (or its equivalent). Clamp up the traversing clamp, remove the tower from the crosshead, and replace the gun, which will now be pointing in the required direction.

Four guns, reasonably close together, can be laid for direction by this method in less than five minutes. The accuracy is the same as can be obtained by any other method in which the compass is employed, and the operation is performed without anyone leaving the gun position.

The instrument is strongly made, and could be issued ready for use without any adjustments being necessary other than placing the compass correctly on the table, an operation of a few seconds only. Opinions of Machine Gun Officers are requested as to whether this instrument should be recommended for issue.

(30) LUMINOUS AUXILIARY AIMING MARK.*

In accordance with the suggestion put forward by the Corps Machine Gun Officers at the Conference on March 21st, trials have been carried out with an Aiming Mark consisting of a disc 1 inch in diameter mounted on a steel rod and coated with luminous paint. (BALMAINS, best quality).

Without radium sights, it was impossible to lay on this disc, even though it was only 4 yards from the gun.

Using the radium sights, however, it was possible for an expert gunner to lay accurately on the disc (placed 6 yards from the gun) for a period of about a quarter of an hour after the disc had been exposed to the light of an electric torch. Time required to lay—about 15 secs. After quarter of an hour, however, the luminosity diminished to such an extent that it was almost impossible to maintain a constant aim.

The elevation errors of different firers varied between 5 minutes and 60 minutes after a period of 20 minutes had elapsed from the time of exposure. The time required to lay was also much longer. From this it would seem that the disc is not of much value as a luminous Auxiliary Aiming Mark unless it can be constantly resuscitated every 15 minutes or thereabouts, or unless a stronger luminous paint is obtainable.

Further suggestions are required from Corps Machine Gun Officers; meanwhile experiments on other lines are being carried out at the Machine Gun Training Centre.

(31) Wire Cutting by Machine Guns.

Experiments have been carried out in wire cutting, with the result that the following opinion has been formed:—

It is possible for machine guns to cut a path through thick wire, provided:
  (a) That a large amount of ammunition can be employed.
  (b) That the guns can be brought up close enough (300 yards to 500 yards).

But it is very doubtful whether the enemy would allow condition (b).

Section D,—TESTS.

(32) Provisional Report of Endurance Test of ·303 Vickers Gun.*

  i. Gun, Vickers ·303 No. L. 6273 practically new, had only fired about 500 rounds previously.
  ii. Tripod Mark IV. New and rigid.
  iii. Ammunition G. 16. and R.L.
  iv. The same firer fired the whole test and had the assistance of expert Nos. 2, 3, and 4.
  v. The gun was carefully examined and gauged previous to firing and was found up to standard.
  vi. The weight of the Fusee Spring was $7\frac{1}{2}$ lbs.
  vii. The Muzzle Cup was attached in accordance with the instructions laid down.

The total time occupied in the test was 60 minutes 4 seconds.

Rounds Fired.	Belts.
13,750	55

The average rate of fire for the whole period was 229 rounds per minute.

The highest rate of fire for any one belt was 555 rounds per minute.

The slowest rate of fire for any one belt was 405 rounds per minute.

The average rate of fire for the whole period, exclusive of stoppage, was 471 rounds per minute.

The best "runs" of the gun were always obtained immediatery after oiling; the effect of oil appears to last about 4 belts, after that stoppages increase.

For Comparison.

	Belts.	Rounds.	Total Time.	Average Rate.
After Oiling.	7—10	1,000	2 min. 28 sec.	406
	18—21	1,000	2 ,, 24 ,,	417
	26—29	1,000	2 ,, 23 ,,	420
	46—50	1,250	3 ,, 16 ,,	382
Lack of Oil.	51—55	1,250	5 ,, 10 ,,	242
	40—43	1,000	5 ,, 35 ,,	179

The total time was divided as follows:—

(i.) Changing Belts, 54 times, 7 min. 21 sec. Average $8\frac{1}{8}$ secs.
(ii.) Refilling water and oiling. 7 times, 12 min. 16 sec. Average 1 min. 45 sec.
(iii.) Remedying stoppages. 57 times, 11 min. 17 sec. Average 12 sec.
(iv.) Actual rapid firing. (Aimed bursts) 29 min. 10 sec.

The stoppages were as follows:—

1st position, 7. Total time occupied in remedying, 22 sec. Average 3 sec.
2nd position, 3. Total time occupied in remedying, 68 sec. Average 23 sec.
3rd position, 23. Total time occupied in remedying, 436 sec. Average, $18\frac{1}{2}$ sec.
4th position, 24. Total time occupied in remedying, 151 sec. Average $6\frac{1}{3}$ sec.

The frequency of the 3rd position stoppages and the disproportionate time to remedy deserves notice. The front cover catch, if in good order and holding well, cannot be opened when the gun is hot without burning the knuckles of No. 1's fingers. The clearing plug had to be employed to lever it open and it is estimated that almost half the total time occupied in stoppages was due to this cause alone.

The amount of water used was 6 gallons, 8 pints for 55 belts, this works out at approximately one pint per belt, and starting all cold it would not be advisable to fire the gun for more than 2,000 rounds before refilling.

The total amount of oil used was $\frac{1}{2}$ pint: the oil in the handles lasted 17 belts, or 4,250 rounds, by which time the oil was used up and the brushes rendered useless owing to the heat of gun charring hairs. The oil can was found quicker and more efficient.

Unavoidable stoppage.
i. One lock spring was broken in the 38th belt.
ii. Packing gland loose ½ turn at conclusion of 45th belt.

The gun was examined at the conclusion of the trial.

Barrel. Lead plug entered 2 inches.
·310 ,, ,, ,, breech 4 inches.
·308 ,, ,, ,, ,, $7\frac{1}{2}$,,
·307 ,, ,, ,, ,, $8\frac{1}{2}$,,
·303 ,, ,, would not enter muzzle.

The "lead" was eroded considerably, but there were only slight traces of nickelling in the barrel.

The barrel retains about ¾ of its rifling and is considered still serviceable.

The working parts of the gun showed no signs of wear.

The packing in the glands and cannelure were found intact.

The muzzle cup was found difficult to remove, and the front cone was filled up with metallic deposit leaving no clearance between muzzle cup and itself when recoiling portions were forward.

A more complete examination of the gun will be carried out at Enfield.

Noticeable quantities of nickel were blown out in the 41st, 46th, and 51st belt.

The flash appeared to vary in intensity, possibly due to different ammunition.

Muzzle cup gave no trouble and was in perfect order at the termination of the trial.

The firer complained of fatigue in the hands: the ball of the thumb becomes slightly numbed as a result of—
(a) Continued pressure. (b) Vibration.

It is considered that the endurance of the gun will outlast the endurance of any one firer, and when the trial was stopped at the end of the first hour, the gun was running rather better than at the beginning, and might have continued indefinitely until the barrel was worn out.

(33) MARK II. MUZZLE CUPS.

Mark II. muzzle cups have been found very satisfactory. Care must be taken that the thread is clean and free from oil before screwing on the cup, otherwise the oil carbonizes, and it is next to impossible to remove the cup.

The cup should be screwed on until it cannot be moved by hand, but without forcing it, and should be tested after every fifth belt or so.

(34) REPORT ON TRIALS WITH TRACER AMMUNITION FIRED FROM VICKERS' GUN.*

(1) *Object.*—The following questions were raised at the conference of Corps Machine Gun Officers, held at the Machine Gun School, France, on the 21st March, 1917 :—

   (a) What were the value and uses of " Tracer Bullets " for—
      (i.) Ranging purposes and best methods of employment ?
      (ii.) Anti-aircraft defences ?

   (b) Can bullets be obtained with the same range and trajectory as the Mark VII. ammunition ?

It was decided to carry out some trials at the Machine Gun Training Centre, and obtain some information on the subject.

(2) *Ammunition.*—The following Tracer ammunition was obtained :
    5,000 rounds S.P.G., old make, returned from France, dated July, 1916.
    300 rounds S.P.G., new manufacture, dated 31st March, 1917.

(3) *Firing Tables.*—

   1ST SERIES.—Range : 900 yards.
                Weather : Fine with bright sunshine.

   To determine—
     (i.) Ranging powers.
     (ii.) Visibility.
     (iii.) Value in overhead fire.

RESULT.

   (i.) Unsatisfactory ; the bullet only traced for about 750 yards, and facility for observation was not increased to any material extent.

   (ii.) The trace could be clearly observed as far as it went, viz. : 750 yards, so any value pertaining to it beyond that distance is lost. The most suitable position for observation is, apparently, directly behind the gun. Fire was directed on to an intermediate target at a range unknown to the firer (actually 700 yards); the target was quickly picked up, but it is doubtful whether this was due to the tracer ammunition any more than to the skill of the firer.

   (iii.) There is no value in the use of tracer ammunition for overhead fire, but actual danger to our troops; although no hits were registered on the targets representing the friendly troops, yet many shots or portions of bullets were seen to strike the ground between the gun and friendly troops. This has never occurred when no tracer ammunition was mixed with the ordinary S.A.A.

2ND SERIES.—Range : 600 yards.
Weather : As above.

To determine how far the use of tracer bullets will give away the gun position.

RESULT.

The gun was fired from the edge of a wood with observers 300 yards to a flank and 200 yards to the front.

Although the observers did not know the exact position of the gun, yet after the first few rounds this was easily located, as the trace of the bullet was plainly visible during the first 200 yards of its flight, and this trace would be visible from a much greater distance away from the gun.

(4) *Summary.*—It was clear to all those who witnessed these trials that the use of tracer ammunition for ground work has a negative value, and is a positive danger, either by day or night.

It is possible that for the purposes of demonstrating the trajectory of short ranges, or for bands of fire it would have a practical value, and would make a most interesting demonstration.

In every case when the old tracer ammunition was fired (10 months old) the results were most unreliable and misleading. The new tracer ammunition about 1 month old appeared to give an accurate trace, but was still liable to give prematures (showing brilliant flashes at the gun muzzle).

(5) The S.P.G. brand is the latest and best type of tracer we have.

A tracer has been tried which was claimed to trace up to 1,400 yards, but this does not give a true trajectory owing to the rapid loss in weight and consequent loss in velocity.

To obtain a bullet which would trace to the maximum range of 2,800 yards, the bullet would have to burn for 16 secs., lose no weight, and be sufficiently brilliant to enable the observer to watch its flight throughout the whole of the trajectory.

The present S.P.G. bullet burns for about $1\frac{1}{4}$ secs.

(6) In these trials various proportions of tracer bullets to ordinary Mark VII. were tried, ranging from 1 in 2 to 1 in 20. The conclusions arrived at are not affected in any way.

(35) LIFE OF BARRELS, AND ACCURACY.

It is reported that the average life for a barrel which is used for indirect fire is about 21,500 rounds before its accuracy is seriously impaired.

(36) AMMUNITION TEST.

From a careful classification of missfires and thick rims in a large quantity of ammunition fired, it would seem that the following is the order of merit :—

1st. "K."
2nd. "KN."
3rd. "R."
4th. "KL."
5th. "E."
6th. "G."
7th. "J."
8th. "U" and "US."

Section E.—GENERAL.

(37) INDIRECT OVERHEAD FIRE SAFETY LIMITS.

(a) It has been suggested that the present safety limits for barrage fire are excessive with well-trained machine gun companies, and that the following should be substituted, giving minimum clearances at each 100 yards distance of own troops from the gun, instead of the sudden jumps of 20, 40, and 80 yards hitherto employed :—

Range to Troops.	Clearance required.
600 and below	11 yards.
700	13 ,,
800	15 ,,
900	17 ,,
1000	20 ,,
1100	23 ,,
1200	27 ,,
1300	31 ,,
1400	35 ,,
1500	40 ,,
1600	46 ,,
1700	53 ,,
1800	60 ,,
1900	69 ,,
2000	80 ,,

(b)* With reference to the above suggestions, it is pointed out by M.G.T.C. that the safety clearances of 20, 40, and 80 yards for distances of 1,000 and under, 1,000—1,500, and 1,500—2,000 yards respectively have not been reduced.

It appears to be the general opinion that these clearances are excessive, and the following table of clearances is, therefore, put forward for consideration, with a view to its adoption at an early date.

The clearances are based on the following allowances:—

(i.) A possible plus or minus 5 per cent. error in estimating the distance to own troops (map error, etc.).

(ii.) A possible variation of − 30 minutes in the angle of fire (quadrant angle) due to play in tripod joint pins, bad "holding," etc.

(iii.) Half the height of the vertical axis of the cone, at each distance of own troops from the gun position (because clearances are calculated to centre shot of cone).

(iv.) One per cent. of the distance of our own troops from the gun position added to (iii.) as ultimate clearance, supposing that the maximum errors of (i.) and (ii.) had been made.

TABLE OF SAFETY CLEARANCES (SUGGESTED) FOR INDIRECT OVERHEAD FIRE.

Distance of own Troops from Gun.	Minimum Clearance in Yards.
500 and under	11
600	13
700	15
800	17
900	19
1000	**22**
1100	25
1200	28
1300	31
1400	34
1500	**37**
1600	40
1700	43
1800	46
1900	49
2000	**52**

Opinions from Corps Machine Gun Officers are requested upon this.

(38) MESSAGE PAD.

The message form shown below has been found of great value in recent fighting. It is proposed to print these forms in pads of the same size as A.F., C.2121, for issue to Machine Gun Companies. Any suggested additions or amendments should be forwarded to O.C. Publications Branch, Machine Gun Training Centre, England, as soon as possible.

Message No..........................

To O.C...........................Company, M.G.C.

1. I am at ....

2. I need ammunition.
   ,, water.
   ,, Very lights.
   ,, spare parts.

3. Counter-attack forming at ....

4. I am in touch with ....on right
   ,, ,, ,, ... on left

5. I am not in touch on right./left.

6. No troops are in front of me at ....

7. I am shelled from .... by own / enemy artillery.

8. Hostile Battery   active at..
   ,, Machine Gun   ,, ...
   ,, Trench Mortar ,, ...

(*Space for messages*).—

Time.......................... Name and Rank...................................
Date... No...............Section.
Map Reference..,.....................Company............M.G.C.

Part III.—Machine Gun Intelligence of Foreign Countries.

Section A.—TACTICS.

(39) TACTICAL HANDLING.

A prisoner, who had been in the "Somme" battle, stated that, as a rule, forward guns were used in the way that our Lewis guns are used. Reserve guns were kept in rear, and did not come into action until the front line broke. Special detachments of machine gun marksmen were used for indirect fire, and were handled by higher formations.

In trench warfare there appears to be an absence of co-ordination, and targets had not been allotted. He seldom saw his officers, and it was left to the N.C.O. to fire where and when he liked.

Prisoner stated that in his company, three machine guns were in the front, two in the support line, and one in rear.

This was not in accordance with instructions issued, which distinctly say that machine guns should rarely be in the front line.

No special emplacement or cover were made, and the guns were moved about from place to place.

He had not been instructed in the use of any gun other than his own.

He stated that our machine gun fire on roads and communication trenches was effective.

(40) EXPERIENCE OF THE FIGHTING AT VERDUN.

(*Extracts from a German Document, signed by Hindenburg.*)

The serious and regrettable reverses sustained at Verdun during October and December have led me to issue the following orders:—

(1) CONSTRUCTION OF DEFENCES.

The principles laid down in the text book "Construction of Defences" (Stellungsbau) have proved sound. Single lines of trenches do not suffice. A fortified zone, organized in depth, must be constructed, allowing of a stubborn defence of an area even after the capture of fragments of its lines of defence.

The rearward portion of this zone will, therefore, consist of a system of strong points, machine gun nests, &c., merging towards the front into an increasingly closer meshed network of trenches. The individual trenches, machine gun nests, &c., must afford each other mutual flanking support.

The front line trench cannot be too thinly held. Distribution in depth is essential, even for a company. Each strong point must have its definite garrison which will be responsible for holding it. Only isolated machine guns will be taken into the front line trench; they will usually be kept in carefully selected positions behind the front line, concealed and posted chequer-wise, frequently in hollows, which are difficult to detect from the air and cannot be reached by the artillery; their main task is to open a surprise flanking fire on an enemy who has broken through. The operation of bringing machine guns into positions, and relieving them, will be specially supervised.

(41) GERMAN RUSES.

The following ruses have been reported:—
- (a) Trench boards (*new* in every case) on fire step, which detonated grenades when trodden on.
- (b) A dozen stick grenades to be fired by means of a wire attached to a sandbag, which had to be moved before the door of a dug-out could be opened.
- (c) Charge in chimney, with length of fuse attached, which would be ignited if a fire were lighted.
- (d) Detonators in lumps of coal.
- (e) Book on table, with wire down leg of table; charge would fire if book were lifted.
- (f) A blown-in entrance to a dug-out is not always a safety sign. Charges may be concealed in the unblown portions. They are generally crudely-arranged contact charges.
- (g) A shovel stuck into the side of a dug-out between the timbers which, when removed, pulled a wire which exploded a mine.
- (h) A French stove with stove-pipe dismantled, one wire attached to leg of stove and the other to stove-pipe near by. When the stove-pipe is picked up a mine is fired.
- (i) A charge of 2,000 lbs. of cordite in a seemingly dead end of a gallery of a dug-out, and connected to ordinary telephone wire. Face of the gallery made up to look like undisturbed ground with pick marks in it.
- (j) A window-weight suspended by fine cord stretched across the entrance to a dug-out. On a man entering, the cord would be broken, and the weight fall into a box of detonators in connection with a charge of explosives.
- (k) Several charges found in dug-outs placed behind the lining. The only visible sign was that in removing the sets the tenon had been out, and on replacement had to be held in place by small wedges.
- (l) A cavity hollowed out under the road, leaving only the crust. An 8 in. shell placed in the cavity with a contact fuse arranged to fire should the road be depressed at all.
- (m) Barricades have been found constructed of farm implements and brushwood, with stick-bombs attached to wires inter-twined in the barricade.
- (n) The badge of a German soldier's cap, attached to a piece of string or wire, which, when raised from the ground, caused an explosion.

(o) Artificial flowers, bits of evergreen, pieces of shell, or a bayonet on the floor or walls of a dug-out, which when lifted ignited a charge which blew the entrance in.
(p) Pieces of wood, having the appearance of a hand-rail, beside steps down a dug-out, had wires with an electric spark attachment running to an explosive charge fastened to them.
(q) Attempts are being made by the enemy to conceal their true order of battle, as in ST. PIERRE VAAST WOOD and elsewhere numbers of old coats, etc., bearing shoulder straps of regiments, known not to be in the area, have been found.

GERMAN AUTOMATIC DETONATING DEVICE
USED IN CONNECTION WITH EXPLOSIVE CHARGES LEFT IN DUG-OUTS, BILLETS & ELSEWHERE.

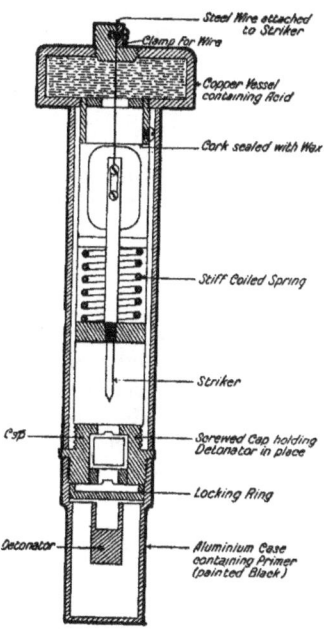

Sectional Elevation.

Section B.—EQUIPMENT.

(42) *The German "Maxim, 1908-15" Light Machine Gun (see plate).*

A very portable weapon which can be used as an automatic rifle. If necessary, one man can bring and keep this gun in action.

Main differences from 1908 model :—

Weight and Length.—Weight with barrel casing filled, 42¾ lbs. Total length, 4 feet 7 inches.

Water Jacket.—Reduced in size. Capacity of jacket reduced from 7 pints to about 5¼ pints.

Breech Casing.—Much lighter, and cut away in the upper rear and lower front portions. Ejector tube abolished. Ejection takes place through an outlet in the front part of breech casing.

Improvised Support takes the place of the sledge carriage. It is made of a mild steel fork, braced at a height of about 4 inches from the ground and finished off by two spades with soles. Elevation is very limited; it is obtained by the action of the fastening collar on the water jacket. Weight of support and fastening collar, about 6¼ lbs.

Stock.—The stock, which is about 12 inches long, is in place of the handles of the rear crosspiece. It has a fluted surface to grip the firer's shoulder.

Revolver Grip is screwed on to the trigger guard, which is rivetted on to the bottom plate. The fluted trigger is placed under the bottom plate and acts directly on the trigger bar. Its movement is controlled by the safety catch, which, when in position "S" (Sicherbeit), checks the backward movement of the trigger. The trigger bar is kept in the forward position by a spring.

Sling.—Attached to the butt stock and to a collar on the water jacket. Used for carrying the gun on a man's back.

Sights.—Different from those on the 1908 model machine guns. Back sight has sight notch on the left. Fore sight of triangular shape, adjustable.

Muzzle Attachment.—The zinc disc, which in the 1908 model machine gun is placed in front of the vent holes through which the gases escape, is abolished. A cup-shaped cylinder, screwed on to a nut, forms a second combustion chamber outside the first. This cylinder also delays the escape of the gases, and thus prolongs their action and allows them to complete their combustion.

There is a belt-box support of T-shaped iron, fixed to the right sideplate at the height of the feed block.

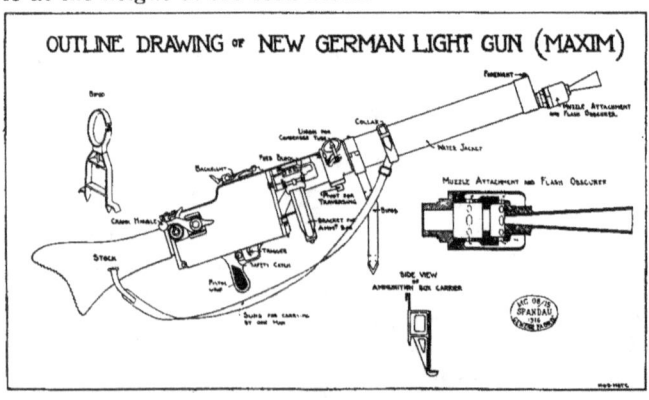

Section C.—ORGANISATION.

(43) REDUCTION OF BATTALION STRENGTHS.
(Translation of captured German document).

In agreement with the Supreme Army Command and with the War Ministries of Bavaria, Saxony and Wurttemburg, it has been decided that :—

As soon as each company has been equipped with 3 light machine guns, the war establishment of infantry and Jager battalions on the western front will be fixed at :—

650 men fit for field service and
100 men fit for garrison or labour employment.

(44) M.G. ORGANISATION.
Examination of German machine gunner of 3rd M.G. Coy. 107th R.I.R., captured on 5th March, 1917.

Prisoner was a reservist, fairly reliable, but rather below average intelligence.

He stated that the M.G. companies are integral parts of the battalion and are numbered by the battalion number. The men wear no distinguishing badge.

The machine gunners are recruited in the same way as other men of the regiment with the exception of the No. 1, who is specially trained at a M.G. school in Germany, the depot of the original M.G. organisation before the regimental system was started.

The ordinary machine gunner undergoes a four weeks course of training.

Section D.—GENERAL.

(45) GAS ATTACK BY THE BRITISH ON THE FRENCH FRONT NEAR NIEUPORT.
(From a deserter).

He stated that the enemy suffered 1,500 casualties (700 dead) and that the gas was so strong that, after the attack, deserter's company could not unlock the bolts of their rifles; all metal arms and equipment of his battalion were rendered unserviceable and handed into store.

(46) GROUPING FIRE WITH ALL CLAMPS LOOSE (Punkt-Feuer).
(Translation from a German document).

This is sustained fire with loose clamps, when the No. 1 takes an aim and maintains that aim as best he can upon the target.

It is employed for shooting at narrow targets such as hostile machine guns, artillery, etc., when the fire director wishes to get observation of fire.

Experience in this war has, however, shown us that this form of fire is valuable for much more general purposes.

The extremely narrow cone obtained by fixed clamp grouping cannot be used effectively against small targets, being too small even when long bursts of, say, 250 rounds are fired.

Compared with grouping fire where elevating and traversing clamps are firmly fixed, the cone has become considerably larger, but its breadth is not yet sufficient to be effective against small targets under battle conditions, when observation is either impossible or extremely difficult.

No fire director in his senses will fire a burst of 250 rounds, if he is not sure of obtaining some effect by observation.

If the target is engaged with fixed traversing but loose elevating gear, the size of the cone will not alter at all laterally, and only very slightly vertically.

Therefore, to enlarge the cone *it is essential to slacken the traversing clamp*.

If No. 1 is an inexperienced shot, or if there is practically no observation possible, the cone becomes considerably enlarged.

It can be made narrower of course by tightening the traversing clamp, or by packing the traversing gear, so that any tendency of the gun to jump laterally is eliminated.

This however would interfere with the traversing of the gun. A compromise would be the wisest plan.

In actual warfare long straight lines are not by any means always available as targets, and often only single heads are visible at intervals, which hardly justify long bursts of fire.

But nevertheless these heads must be kept down by M.G. fire. An observer should be continually on the watch for single heads with his glasses, and as soon as one appears, give the order for a burst of fire—from 10 to 30 rounds usually is sufficient so that no enemy be rash enough to show his head again.

As these heads are generally those of Officers or Section Commanders, the expenditure of ammunition is well justified. This method of fire is best suited to sweep long lines of cover which cannot be observed at all accurately. All spots where the enemy show themselves ought to be swept from time to time with short bursts of fire at certain intervals, so that a kind of traversing fire is obtained; the more visible the target the more like a proper traverse this loose clamp grouping fire becomes. Searching in depth can also be employed for the same purpose.

(47) GERMAN ALL ROUND TRAVERSE.

A machine gunner of the 75th I.R. (17th Division), states that the Germans have found the following device for firing over the parapet very useful; a board with a revolving disc in the centre is pegged down on to the parapet, the machine gun is fastened to the disc by one central screw, and fire can thus easily be brought to bear in all directions.

NOTES ON THE HINDENBURG LINE.

(48) THE TRENCHES IN THE VICINITY AND SOUTH OF ST. QUENTIN.

The line is made up of a series of salients and re-entrants, with a view to the intensive use of machine guns.

The line is generally sited on the reverse slope, but is provided with salients with a view to securing observation.

(49) MACHINE GUN EMPLACEMENTS OUTSIDE TRENCHES.

In the above sector, machine gun emplacements are mostly some 10—20 yards in *front* of the trench, and connected to the main line by two shafts inclined at 45° (or else vertical), these being linked up by means of an underground passage some 20—30 feet below ground.

The mouth of the shaft in front of the trench is extremely small, and is possibly concreted.

This type of emplacement is found also in many cases in the QUEANT Sector, situated outside the trenches, in holes, in or near the wire of the front or support lines, and approached by underground passages.

The appearance of this type of emplacement in air photographs appears to be that of a hole surrounded by a mound of earth. A sketch, enlarged from photo 3 Æ 407, is attached showing some of these emplacements, identified by comparison with a captured map. Such emplacements are also constructed in rear of the support line, as will be seen from the sketch. Though the approach to them is covered for some distance, there usually seems to be a trench in fairly close proximity. The neighbourhood of the support line wire seems to be a favourite position for these machine guns.

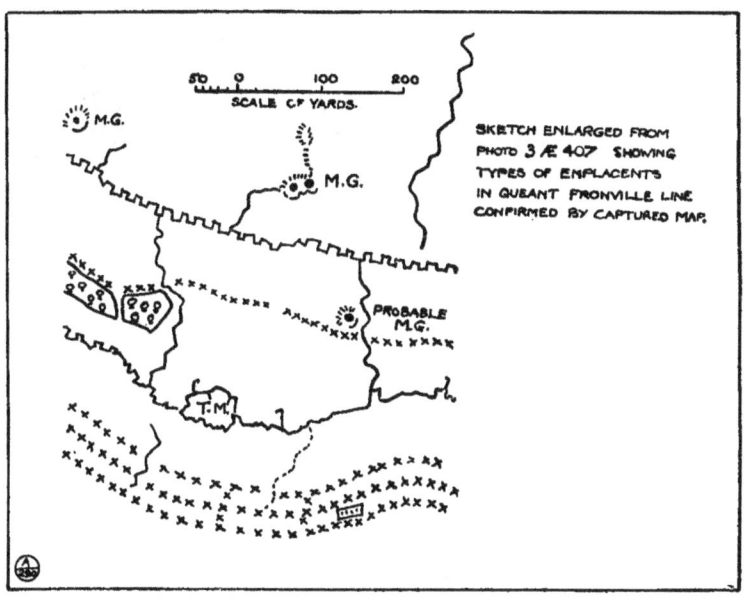

An instance of a type of trench mortar emplacement is also illustrated in the sketch attached. It is constructed in a short length of trench forming a loop in rear of the main line.

Machine gun and trench mortar emplacements of the types referred to above should be carefully looked for. Owing to their isolated positions outside the trench lines, they will require to be dealt with specially, and they are probably sited as much with a view to avoiding damage during a bombardment of the trench line, as to obtaining an improved field of fire.

(50) MACHINE GUN EMPLACEMENTS IN TRENCHES.

In the part of the line south of Fontaine, about U 7, many examples of emplacements may be seen situated in the fire trench itself or slightly in advance of it. Though some of these have a loop of trench immediately behind them, they would appear more likely to contain machine guns than trench mortars, as they are in most cases protected by a belt of sunk wire at close range, an obstacle which would not be of the same value to a trench mortar as to a machine gun. A sketch is attached.

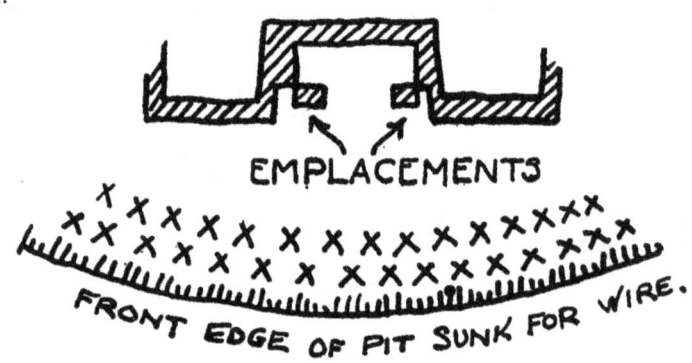

A similar system is reported on the front between Fontaine and Heninel.

For the defence of the line in this sector, the Germans apparently relied on a series of ferro-concrete machine gun posts at intervals of from 80 to 150 yards, sited to flank the angles of the wire.

These emplacements were constructed for two machine guns to fire over the parapet, while the observer was protected by steel loopholes with a trap overhead in the steel plate for a periscope.

Accommodation for the gun crews was provided between the gun emplacements.

Similar emplacements occur in the support line, generally sited in a main communication trench, which forks round their position.

(The principle of accommodating the garrison and guns of the defence in well-defined strong points, which can be identified on air photographs, will undoubtedly favour the attacker, as destructive fire can be limited to these objectives, and the field barrage will prevent them being manned until the last moment).

The emplacements are strong enough to resist all fire, except from shells of 8-inch and above.

(51) Dug-outs.

Troops were working hard on the dug-outs on 7th March, 1917; they were not nearly completed. The dug-outs are of the usual type, very deep, with four entrances, and are distributed at the rate of two per company sector of 150 yards. In each dug-out a number of boards have been taken out at a height of one yard from the floor, the earth has been removed and an explosive charge placed in the cavity ready for ignition by time-fuse. The boards have then been replaced and marked with crosses in blue or lead pencil. Ammunition dug-outs have been concreted.

(52) Entanglements.

Between Fontaine and Heninel, wire entanglements are of a serrated pattern, and so constructed that the sides of the angles are flanked by fire.

Sunken wire entanglements were also met with in certain parts of the line. Three rows were usually found in front of both the front and support lines. No saps or listening posts had been constructed.

(One of the main features of the system of wire entanglements is the distance (varying up to 200 yards) between the front row of wire and the front line trench. An advance by night, to dig in under cover of the enemy's wire or to destroy it by torpedoes, is therefore feasible).

No. 618.   21-6-17.   250.
Publications Branch,
Machine Gun Training Centre.

CONFIDENTIAL.

$\frac{40}{\frac{W.O.}{4293}}$

FOR OFFICIAL USE ONLY.

SUMMARY OF MACHINE GUN INTELLIGENCE

No. 2.

Issued by the General Staff.

JUNE, 1917.

PRINTED AT THE MACHINE GUN SCHOOL, MACHINE GUN TRAINING CENTRE.
UNDER THE AUTHORITY OF HIS MAJESTY'S STATIONERY OFFICE,

CONTENTS.

Part I. Training.

Section *a*. Personnel.
,, *b*. Transport.
,, *c*. Co-operation.
,, *d*. Gas.
,, *e*. Operations—Notes on.
,, *f*. General.

Part II. Technical.

Section *a*. Equipment.
,, *b*. Demonstrations.
,, *c*. Experiments.
,, *d*. Tests.
,, *e*. General.

Part III.
Machine Gun Intelligence of Foreign Countries.

Section *a*. Tactics.
,, *b*. Equipment.
,, *c*. Organization.
,, *d*. General.

NOTE.—With the exception of those paragraphs marked with an asterisk, the information contained in this Summary has been extracted from reports received from General Headquarters of Expeditionary Forces.

PART I.—TRAINING.

Section A.—PERSONNEL.

(53) NOTES FROM A CORPS CONCERNING TACTICAL TRAINING.

Reports received from FRANCE on the VIMY RIDGE battle lay stress on the importance of the Machine Gun Companies being as highly trained tactically as they are technically. They tend to show that the tactical training needs attention.

The training in the use of the compass has improved, but requires to be developed.

Section B.—TRANSPORT.

(54) MOVEMENT OF TRANSPORT DURING AN ADVANCE.

The transport lines of a Machine Gun Company should be pushed forward as soon, and as far as possible, during an advance. Opportunities occur for using fighting limbers, and especially pack mules. Owing to the necessarily congested condition of traffic, these cannot be up in time if the transport lines are several miles away. The nearer the transport is to the Company Commander the better will he be able to utilise it, and so reduce the necessity of repeated calls on the men to carry guns, ammunition, stores, etc.

Section C.—CO-OPERATION.

(55) CO-OPERATION WITH STOKES MORTARS.

A combined shoot with two Stokes Mortars was carried out with success. The two mortars took a certain section of the enemy trench at the flanks and worked inwards. The enemy in between attempted to bolt over the open, and were successfully dealt with by the machine gun. On several occasions during the recent operations, many good targets were obtained in this manner.

(56) CO-OPERATION WITH ROYAL ENGINEERS.

In one instance, a party of sappers was detailed to accompany the machine gunners in the advance. This proved most effective. A narrow trench, 10 feet deep, was dug, in which the detachment lay all day throughout a very heavy bombardment without any casualties.

Section D.—GAS.
NIL.

Section E.—OPERATIONS : Notes on.

(57) THE FOLLOWING EXTRACTS HAVE BEEN MADE FROM REPORTS RECEIVED ON THE OPERATIONS LEADING TO THE CAPTURE OF THE VIMY RIDGE :—

Four phases were considered and legislated for in Corps Orders during the operations leading to the capture of the VIMY RIDGE :—

- (a) The employment of machine guns for harassing fire previous to zero day.
- (b) The employment of machine guns for supporting fire during the attack, and the establishment of a defensive barrage for each definite phase of the operation.
- (c) The employment of guns detailed to advance with the assaulting Brigades.
- (d) The employment of guns in the consolidation and holding of the ground after its capture.

(a) *Harassing Fire.*

Prisoners captured during the month of March stated that movement was frequently restricted to communication trenches, movement overland being difficult and dangerous on account of machine gun fire. The scarcity of overland tracks, within machine gun range, seen on photographs taken when the snow was on the ground, appears to corroborate these statements.

It is probable that restricting the traffic to the trenches caused congestion, and interfered with the carrying parties. It also added to the effectiveness of the artillery night-firing, field guns being used to enfilade communication trenches known to be in use.

The traffic on trench railways was also seriously hampered by machine gun fire.

There can be no doubt the results sought by harassing fire, *viz.* :—

- (i.) Lowering of the efficiency of the working parties ;
- (ii.) Increasing the difficulties of transport of material and trench mortar ammunition ;
- (iii.) Deterioration of the enemy morale ;

were in a large measure attained during that period.

The following Lessons were deduced:—

Machine gun fire at night, when the targets are selected with care, is an appreciable factor in the deterioration of the enemy's morale.

It is not so much the number of casualties caused by this fire, but rather the precautions that individuals and parties are compelled to take to avoid these casualties, that have a very depressing effect.

By compelling the enemy to use the communication trenches almost exclusively, and interfering with the operation of trench railways, congestion is sure to result, carrying becomes difficult, and the repair of trenches and wire, during the period of systematic bombardment, is seriously hampered. Artillery were also reasonably certain of causing casualties with well directed night-firing on communication trenches known to be much used.

The number of trench mortars captured during the subsequent operations indicated that the decrease of trench mortar activity was not due to the withdrawal of these weapons, but rather to the difficulty of bringing sufficient ammunition forward.

Close liaison between the Intelligence Officers, the artillery, trench mortars and machine gunners, gave very appreciable results during the period under consideration, and led to the adoption of a comprehensive, systematic, and relentless programme for harassing the enemy.

Whatever method of firing is adopted, the best results can only be obtained by the closest co-operation between the Intelligence Officers and the Divisional Machine Gun Officer.

In making provisions for active operations in any sector, the wear and tear of machine guns, during the preliminary stages, should be taken into consideration, and steps taken to ensure an adequate supply of spare parts, more especially of spare barrels.

(b) *Supporting Fire and Defensive Barrages during the Attack.*

If the hostile artillery is active, considerable time may elapse before the work of consolidation is sufficiently advanced to be of great value in case of counter-attack. The Germans endeavour at all times to take advantage of these conditions to deliver immediate counter-attacks overland with their local reserves. These immediate counter-attacks have often been successful.

In addition to the means already employed to guard against these contingencies, it was proposed to provide, at each definite phase of the attack, a protective barrage of machine gun fire of sufficient density to break down immediate counter-attacks delivered overland.

It was calculated that the density required was obtained by allotting one machine gun to every 50 yards of front. It was also determined that frontal, or nearly frontal, fire was required to neutralize a zone of ground sufficiently deep to prove effective. The short range of the machine guns, the difficulty generally experienced in maintaining communications otherwise than by runners, and the fact that visual observation is very seldom obtainable, are so many factors preventing the localisation of the fire zones as practised by the artillery.

Therefore, to be effective, the machine gun barrage must be continuous, and fire must be applied instantly, on as wide a front as possible, upon the S.O.S. being sent up.

The large number of machine guns to be used for barrage purposes were found from :—

(i.) Part of the machine guns of the Brigades in support or reserve.

(ii.) Divisional Machine Gun Companies, and Motor Machine Gun Batteries.

(iii.) The surplus machine guns of the assaulting Brigades, not required during the attack and the early stages of consolidation.

It is out of the question to reduce, for the purpose of setting up a machine gun barrage organization, the number of the machine guns actually required by the assaulting troops, but the narrow frontage of the formations attacking, and the liberal allowance of Lewis guns with the battalions, leaves room for the employment of a comparatively small number of machine guns with the assaulting troops for early consolidation. *(The method of attack behind a creeping barrage practically precludes the employment of machine guns with the assaulting troops for supporting fire, and when the opportunity arises, it is seized much more quickly by the Lewis guns).*

Reports had shown that machine gun barrages had proved very successful in the Somme fighting, and, as the infantry became familiar with, and gained confidence in machine gun overhead fire, additional tasks were given to machine gun batteries.

In the preparation for the capture of Vimy Ridge, it was considered that supporting fire was needed on the entire corps front, at every step of the attack, owing to the great number, the strength, and the commanding position of most of the trenches.

The Operation: Fire and Moves.—The operation was carried out materially as planned. The moves were carried out, and supporting fire and barrages applied in accordance with the Fire Organization Orders.

A small number of guns were knocked out when crossing the hostile barrage, but the losses were much below what was expected, and did not interfere to any extent with the efficiency of the organization and co-operation.

The targets of the guns destroyed were automatically covered by the other guns of the batteries, and the rate of fire speeded up to compensate for the reduction in the number of guns.

Ammunition and Water.—The arrangements made for the carrying forward of the large quantities of ammunition and cooling water required, worked without serious hitch.

Some difficulties were experienced in locating the ammunition dumps, the ground being so badly cut up by shelling. A remedy for this is suggested below.

On the whole, visual signalling did not come up to expectations, partially because the visibility was fair only, and was rendered more difficult by hostile shelling.

Telephonic communication was established in some cases early after the advance, and these were moderately successful.

Control and Liaison.—The Divisions had the control of the guns covering their front. No alterations were to be made, however, to the barrages without the approval of the Corps.

The Brigades exercised the control through the O.C. Groups.

In several instances the Brigades availed themselves of this control to allot secondary targets to the batteries under them, and concentrated fire was brought quickly to bear on points where the enemy was reported concentrating. In two instances it is reported that excellent results were obtained by this method.

A case occurred in which a Group Commander failed to realise the necessity of maintaining effective liaison with the Brigade. This failure led to missing good opportunities to inflict losses on the enemy.

Results Obtained.—The attempt made to support the advance of the infantry by machine gun fire of medium intensity, was very successfully accomplished, notwithstanding the great difficulties which had to be overcome.

Reports show that all Divisions were satisfied with the fire of the machine guns and one Division reported that heavy casualties had been inflicted when the Germans, trying to run away from the artillery barrage, blundered into the machine gun barrage.

SPECIMEN OF FIRE ORGANIZATION ORDER.

No. of Group or Battery	No. of Guns	Composition	Commander	Location	Firing From	Firing To	Target	Rate of Fire	Remarks
6	8	"X" M.G. Coy.	Lieut. "A"	A.3. c. 2.9	0	10	A.5. c. 30.05 to A.5. c. 40.85	3000*	
					11	14	A.5. c. 30.05 to A.5. c. 45.85	,,	
					15	17	A.5. c. 65.05 to A.5. c. 45.85	,,	
					18	20	A.5. c. 70.05 to A.5. c. 65.85	,,	
					21	25	A.5. c. 90.05 to A.5. c. 85.85	,,	
							To Barrage.		
					26	65	A.5. d. 10.05 to A.5. d. 05.85	1500†	
					66	70	A.5. d. 30.25 to A.5. b. 4.1	3000*	

* Per hour per gun.
† Per hour per gun (after first belt continuous).

Ammunition Dumps.—As soon as established, ammunition dumps should be marked with a flapper or a board. Serious difficulties were experienced in locating the dumps after they had been made.

The "battery" positions should also be indicated by a flapper. The carriers find it very difficult to locate the "batteries" when they are not firing.

The Venetian flapper would appear to answer these requirements.

Pack Trains.—The pack trains were a great success. Ammunition was kept plentiful. The amount of ammunition needed could not possibly have been carried forward to the advanced positions by carrying parties. The distance was too long and the going too heavy, and no doubt the casualties to men would have been very severe.

The pack trains went forward as soon as direct observation was denied the enemy. The losses in animals were very moderate.

Movement Forward of the Batteries.—The time and method of moving were left entirely to the discretion of the Officers Commanding the batteries. The Officers, without exception, used great judgment, and were able to pick their way through the barrage with very few casualties. (Five batteries had none.)

Reports tend to show that when moving forward immediately after the attack, the first party should include six carriers in addition to the gunners, so as to be able to move more quickly. Four of these carriers would be, after one trip, available for other work.

Distance of Barrage.—The final barrage must be as close as possible consistent with the safety of our own troops. On rising or fairly level ground, a good guide is the centre line of the artillery barrage. The lowest bullet of the cone of machine gun fire should be just beyond that line.

(c) *Guns detailed to Advance with Assaulting Troops.*

Every effort must be made, as soon as possible after the infantry have reached their objective, to bring the batteries to within 2,000 yards of the final barrage line. The closer the range, the more effective the fire.

In all the Divisions, the movements forward of the machine guns were directed towards the early consolidation of the ground won, and a progressive organization in depth of the defences.

Each machine gun was allotted a definite locality, which was to be reached at a definite stage of the operation. Provisions were made to cover the flanks of the units or formations, or to fill gaps in the line, if they occurred.

The machine gun detachments which went forward with the infantry were able to engage by direct fire at medium or long range, scattered bodies of troops, gun limbers, etc.

(d) *Guns for Consolidation.*

The machine guns are most valuable for the consolidation and defensive organization of the ground won, filling up gaps, and protecting the flanks of units or formations. All this is best done by the machine guns kept in the hands of the Battalion Commanders or the Brigadiers.

These guns should move forward to the point allotted to them progressively, in accordance with the plans made beforehand, as the assaulting troops reach definite lines. This method will ensure that some of the mobile guns will always be available for emergencies until all the objectives are reached and the consolidation is well in hand.

It is desirable that a certain number of machine guns should reach points from which observation is obtainable, very soon after the assaulting troops. Whether these guns should disclose themselves by firing on unimportant, scattered parties, depends entirely on the aspect of the battle.

Defensive Organization.—Regarding the defensive organization of the ground, great importance was attached to the distribution of machine guns in depth. The guns were disposed for close range, flanking fire, and, as far as possible, were to support one another.

In addition, machine guns were to be placed at commanding points to participate in the defence by direct fire at medium range.

This training with the infantry proved of great value, and had the additional advantage of enabling the detachments to obtain a thorough knowledge of every detail of the operation beforehand. Each man knew where he was to go, how to get there, and what duties he was expected to perform on arrival at his allotted position. In several cases, after the loss of their leaders, the men carried on, performing their duty with great dash and exactitude.

Carriers.—The number of ammunition carriers with the machine gun detachment, should be proportionate to the depth of the advance. If the advance exceeds 2,000 yards, it is desirable that six ammunition carriers should start with the detachment.

Old German Trenches.—The general impression is that the machine gun must keep away from old German trenches, and that it is better to get into shell holes or dig in well in front of the old trenches.

(58) LOCATION OF GUNS BY HOSTILE AIRCRAFT.

Artillery shelled our positions heavily. At 11 a.m. on the —, an enemy aeroplane flew over the gun positions at a low altitude and dropped white lights over all the positions. No action followed until 6-30 p.m., when a heavy barrage was directed against the guns causing casualties and putting two guns out of action. As soon as light permitted, these guns were withdrawn on authority from the Brigade. The following night a creeping barrage was placed 200 yards in rear of the evacuated gun positions and crept slowly forward. Had the guns still been in position the majority of the men would have been casualties and the guns destroyed.

(59) COMMUNICATION IN BARRAGE FIRE.

The following system of communications between a Division and the guns on barrage work was found to work satisfactorily.

The D.M.G.O. established his Headquarters in a forward O.P. from whence an excellent view of the whole of the Divisional front could be obtained.

Telephone communication was established to Brigades and Divisions from this O.P. This held good throughout the whole of the operations.

Two runners per Company were told off to remain at these Headquarters, and communication to the two Companies was kept up through these runners.

Throughout the operations communication was kept up and alterations as to barrage work, which were found necessary were carried out successfully.

Section F.—GENERAL.

NIL.

PART II.—TECHNICAL.

Section A.—EQUIPMENT.

(60) AMMUNITION BELTS.

During an advance a great number of belts and belt boxes are lost, and there is difficulty in replacing them. It is of great importance that this should be realized by all ranks, and that every effort should be made to curtail this loss.

(61) UTILISATION OF CAPTURED MACHINE GUNS.

In a successful assault German machine guns and ammunition should at once be collected and the guns got into action to meet an immediate counter-attack. This will increase fire power, and economise in the expenditure of our own ammunition.

Section B.—DEMONSTRATIONS.
NIL.

Section C.—EXPERIMENTS.
NIL.

Section D.—TESTS.
NIL.

Section E.—GENERAL.

(62) VICKERS GUN: ADJUSTMENT OF LENGTH OF CONNECTING ROD.*

The following notes have been received from the makers:—

The two sizes of washers, *viz.:* ·003 and ·005 of an inch, are issued in order to enable the connecting rod to be adjusted finely.

By the use of these sizes in combination, the following adjustments, 3, 5, 6, 8, 9, and 10 thousandths of an inch may be made.

(NOTE.—The adjustment is commonly made with the two washers together. This is sufficient in action, but a fine adjustment might be made subsequently after the gun has been withdrawn. It is not necessary, for any mechanical reason, for the two washers always to be used together).

Part III.—Machine Gun Intelligence of Foreign Countries.

Paragraphs marked thus † are Translations from Captured German Documents.

Section A.—TACTICS.

(63) TACTICAL EMPLOYMENT OF THE NEW GERMAN LIGHT MACHINE GUN ('08/15 pattern).

(a) *Notes translated from the French.*

The appearance of this gun in the field shows that the Germans recognise the ineffectiveness and danger of blockhouses, concrete redoubts, etc., which form too good a target for artillery, and consequently they have adopted a more easily-portable gun, which can be used in shell holes and easily moved from place to place, and thus, in an area however limited, escape the enemy's fire. The greater mobility of the gun also shows the necessity for our infantry—

(i.) To follow step by step the barrage of their own guns.

(ii.) Carefully to clear every corner of conquered territory.

(iii.) To be supplied with all necessary arms and equipment: grenades, light machine guns, etc., etc., to continue neutralising fire as soon as the artillery is compelled to interrupt it.

(b) *Notes translated from the German.*

The '08/15 machine gun* is the most suitable weapon for repulsing an attack. In trench warfare it should, therefore, be placed all along the front line. As it is the principal medium for intensive fire, its proper place is at the most vulnerable points of the position. It is necessary to take this fact into account when selecting the personnel.

---

* *Illustrated in No. 1 of this Summary.*

Possible losses or accidental stoppage of fire must always be provided for. It is a good plan for the greater part of the time, to keep certain guns in reserve, and to attach these to assault troops (*Stosstrupps*), etc. Firing over the parapet will be the general rule. It is always essential for the guns to be got into position very quickly, and the Section Commander is responsible for execution of this order. The Section Commander in the sector where the machine guns are posted, decides what part the machine guns are to take in the engagement. He makes all necessary arrangements for them. He must see that Commanders of infantry groups fulfil the requirements of the gunners in charge, and that the carrying parties come up at the proper time.

As they are specially adapted for supporting assault troops, these guns provide a valuable reserve in a counter-attack. It is absolutely necessary then to attach a carrying party.

In line, and at wide intervals, these guns can follow the waves of infantry and establish themselves easily in the captured position.

(64) GERMAN M.G. TACTICS IN OPEN WARFARE. †

Machine guns are to be used chiefly from rear and flank positions. They are to be employed in the first line exceptionally. Inclusion in the fighting line to be avoided as long as possible.

If the attack succeeds, machine guns are immediately to be brought up into the new positions. There is to be no unnecessary delay in bringing up the machine guns; they are to be rushed up so as to be ready if the enemy makes a counter-attack.

(65) GERMAN M.G. TACTICS IN TRENCH WARFARE. †

Counter-Attack.—Machine guns form a support and protection for the assaulting troops in immediate and methodical counter-attacks, and hold the enemy to his trenches by flanking fire, especially at the moment when the assaulting troops leave their trenches.

The attack, therefore, is to be preceded by machine gun fire from rear or flank positions. These machine guns remain behind when the infantry advances to storm the enemy trenches.

Other machine guns (which have not yet fired) are brought up immediately behind the first wave. They are to be on the spot at the piercing of the enemy line, at the seizure of strong points, and at the clearing of the trenches.

Every machine gun which is brought forward with the advancing infantry requires auxiliary teams—about one group. Their duties are :—

    (a) To carry ammunition.

    (b) To protect the machine gun, particularly on the flank and in the rear.

    (c) To mask the machine gun.

If the auxiliary teams have not been detailed, it is the duty of every Group Commander, on the request of the Gun Captain, to place himself, and his group, at the disposal of the Gun Captain.

The detailing of special assault detachments, which are to deal entirely with machine guns which have not been put out of action, has proved to be very effective. It is necessary to practise the individual detachments—even the individual men—in the tasks allotted to them, *again and again.*

To leave a free field for the counter-attacks of the garrison of the rearward trenches, it is an advantage to arrange the entanglements of the rearward lines chequerwise (see Figure 1). There must be plenty of material ready to block the gaps (knife rests and concertinas).

Ammunition Supply.—Each machine gun of the first line must have a supply of at least 3,000 cartridges; in the second lines 5,000. The supply is provided from the ammunition depôt for Company or Battalion machines, or if need be, by the Machine Gun Company of the Battalion. Further, an ammunition depôt for regimental machine guns has been installed, and is administered by the regimental machine gun Officer. He must have available sufficient reserves of ammunition and material for machine guns, and these reserves must be obtained, by regular requisitions at suitable times.

(66) GERMAN NOTES ON CONSTRUCTION OF MACHINE GUN POSITIONS.†

Care should be taken not to construct positions with too regular an outline, in the area of infantry defence. Such regularity assists both the enemy's destructive fire and his infantry assault. The system of lines of continuous trenches cannot be abandoned, but they should be completed by small concealed irregular works, so designed as to afford mutual support. The system of small strong points, each provided with two machine gun emplacements, and two or more fire trenches, for a garrison of one or two groups, is to be recommended. These trenches should be sited to the flanks, about 30 yards distant from the machine gun emplacement, or echeloned in rear of it. The groups should be provided with shelters in these trenches. Each strong point should be protected by wire entanglements, and connected by wire entanglements to the strong points on either flank. A Commander should be appointed for each strong point. The strong points should be arranged chequerwise, to a depth of from 300—400 yards, over the ground in rear of the first line of resistance.

Built-up machine gun emplacements are soon smashed to pieces, unless they are shell-proof (against heavy artillery). As a rule, the best course is to provide shell-proof shelters for the machine guns, in which they are to be kept until required for action, when they are fired over the parapet.

Covered battle emplacements of concrete, or armour plates, are usually only possible on steep reverse slopes. They must not be conspicuously high.

Rules can hardly be laid down for the construction of shell hole positions during the fight. The obvious procedure here is at once to establish nests of infantry consisting of one or two groups, supported, if circumstances render it advisable, by one or two machine guns, in or behind the line of shell holes occupied, and to construct obstacles and dug-outs for them. By degrees, these nests are linked up with one another and with the switch trenches and retired positions behind them.

Penetration of our lines by the enemy occurs during the battle not only in the case of attacks which are carefully prepared, but it is frequently effected by patrols or small detachments with machine guns which penetrate or sap their way into gaps, particularly in shell hole positions. These small detachments are gradually followed by larger forces. This kind of "nest" is often scarcely noticed to begin with, or does not have sufficient attention paid to it. The seriousness of the situation is usually first recognised when it is too late. Instead of cutting off the "nest" or countering it by a vigorous attack, a methodical attack has to be made.

The alternative machine gun emplacements should be placed in such a way as to offer the same facilities for firing on the same targets as the main emplacement; if this is not done they are not alternative emplacements at all; they are supplementary emplacements from which the guns may fire at other targets.

A supply of hand grenades should be placed in the machine gun dug-outs; it is impossible to give a general rule for the size of this supply, as it depends on the emplacement of the gun. In any case the supply should be so calculated that the gunners can defend themselves with grenades while a breakdown in the gun is being mended, and also, so that grenade fighting may in certain cases enable them to withdraw their gun to the rear.

(67) German Notes on Consolidation of Captured Positions.†

Machine guns should be brought up to the captured position as soon as the infantry has taken it. They must be dug in before a hostile counter-attack is delivered, or the enemy's annihilating fire is opened against the captured position. To bring up machine guns from the lines in rear into the position from which the attack is to be made, and thence to the captured trenches, demands thorough reconnaissance and clear orders as to time, route, objective and duties.

It is advisable to detail a few infantrymen to the machine guns, to act under the order of the section commander. Their duties are: to protect machine gun; to defend it in hand-to-hand fighting (hand grenades); to help in digging in the gun in the captured trench, and to dig connecting trenches in shell hole positions.

(68) German Notes on Machine Gun Organisation in Depth.†

Machine guns, for the employment of which the infantry sector commander (Battalion or Regimental Commander) is responsible, will be spread over the zone of defence on the principle of distribution in depth.

Machine guns should be sparingly employed in the front line trench, where they will generally be prematurely put out of action by the intense bombardment. They will seldom have a good frontal field of fire in such positions, but should rather be placed in such a manner that zones of fire can be formed both in front of, and within the defended area.

In addition to the continuous rearward positions, all localities, for about *nine miles* behind the front line of trenches, must be organized for defence. In connection with this, all available shell-proof cellars must be converted into dug-outs, and provided with the necessary number of entrances. As far as possible, machine gun emplacements should be provided to sweep the ground between the localities.

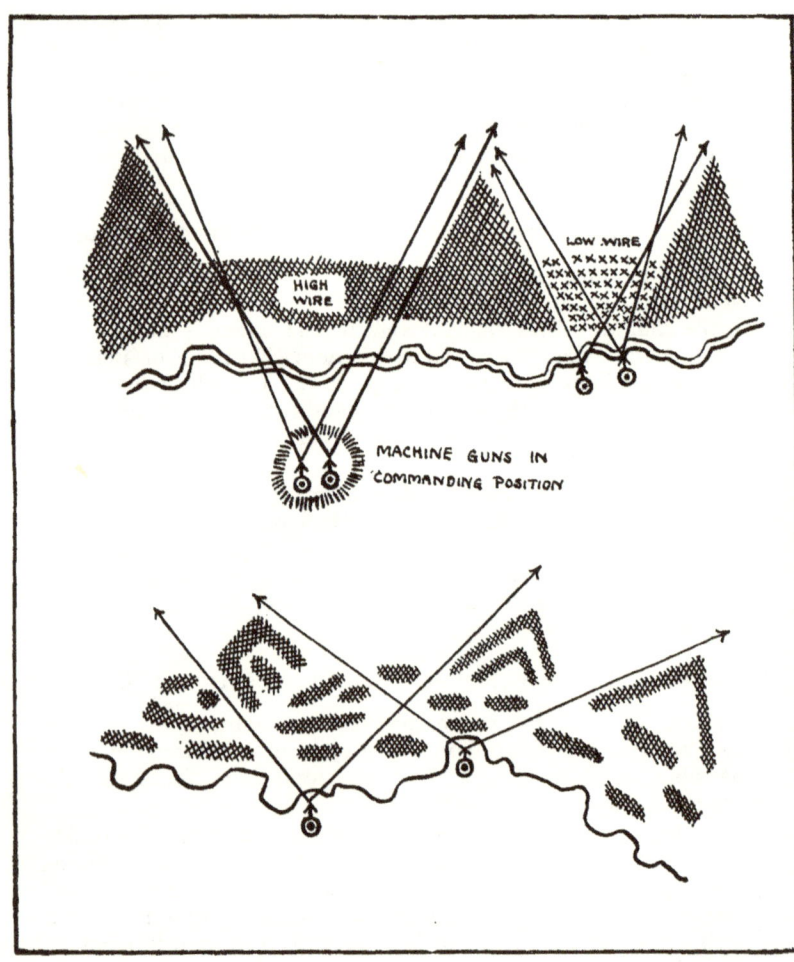

Figure 6.

Entanglements in advance of the front trenches must be as strong as possible, must be erected in regular lines, and must cover wide spaces of ground for 60 to 200 yards in depth. This will force the enemy to an enormous expenditure of ammunition to destroy them, and will ensure that, even after several days' wire cutting, he will find a tangle of wood, wire and iron in front of him.

The flanking of the front line of the entanglements by a suitable arrangement of machine gun fire should not be overlooked. (See Figure 6.)

(69) German Notes on Anti-Tank Defence.†

Phase 1.—The Commencement of the Attack.—It is considered that the barrage and annihilating fire of the heavy and field artillery will, by its intensity, in many cases prevent tanks advancing, and that, therefore, few tanks will reach or cross the German lines.

Phase 2.—Engaging Tanks which have reached the German Line.—(a) The best method to engage such tanks is by means of infantry guns, or close range guns, firing with open sights at short ranges. These are 7.7 cm., or 7.62 cm. (Russian) guns, mounted on low wheels.

(b) In addition, heavy high-angle fire batteries (particularly 15 cm. howitzers) are specially suitable for this task.

These batteries are allotted particular zones as targets, *i.e.*, strips of ground close in front of the German lines, which they can keep under observation, and on which they can register when conditions are quiet.

If a tank enters a zone allotted to such a battery, all guns are turned on to the tank, and salvoes are fired until it is out of action.

(c) Medium and heavy trench mortars can be similarly employed, and must also be allotted definite zones.

Phase 3.—Engaging Tanks which have broken through the German Lines.—(a) These tanks will, in the first instance, be engaged by any battery which they approach (open sights will be used, even with high-angle fire batteries).

(b) In addition, small-calibre guns (5 cm. K.i.P.L.) and (3.7 cm. Sch.Gr.K.) will be allotted to sectors to engage tanks which have broken through.

Anti-tank traps serve no good purpose, unless they are made sufficiently wide (about 8 metres). Special efforts must be made to cause the tanks to turn over sideways.

Battery commanders must construct a great number of traps, especially on the roads.

[*Instruction with Dummy Tanks.*—A captured order, dated 13th April, 1917, shows that the Germans had constructed a model tank, which was lent to units in turn, so as to train the men in aiming at the vulnerable parts. Each unit was given three hours' training with the dummy tank.]

(70) GERMAN INSTRUCTIONS FOR DETACHED MACHINE GUNS.†

The chief task of detached machine guns is to hold up, in the zones of fire allotted to them, hostile troops who have broken through the line, and annihilate them to the last man.

Every man of a detached machine gun team must realise that the longer he holds up the enemy, the sooner will reserves be able to come up to relieve him. Any man who is detailed for duty with a detached machine gun must realise that his superiors are conferring a distinction which shows great reliance on him. From this, it naturally follows that an iron discipline must be maintained voluntarily in the team of a detached machine gun. Recognition and rewards will not be lacking.

The enemy does not know the positions of our detached posts, and everything must, therefore, be done to avoid betraying them, *e.g.*, dense columns of smoke, much traffic, clearly marked tracks, are all to be avoided. When aeroplanes approach, cover must be taken, and men must not stand about to gratify their curiosity.

The machine gun need not necessarily be fired only from its normal emplacement. It is often far better to make use of a hedge, a shell-hole, or the remains of an old wall, than to cling timidly to the concrete emplacement. The ground must be reconnoitred for such alternative positions, and every man must know them. This is all the easier, as the same gun teams will always be sent to the same gun, as far as possible.

Every man must know thoroughly the lie of the land in front of his position, so as to be able to respond to any alarm in any direction, even by night. Gun Captains will daily instruct their men in this from the sketches of the neighbourhood (supplied to them).

Every Gun Captain must know the following: The positions of the guns on his flanks, as well as those of neighbouring regiments, the direction of their fire, and the positions of their emplacements; the exact trace of his own wire; the passages through his own wire; where his own wire is strong and where it is incomplete. Every man must do his utmost to strengthen the wire in front of his position, as it is in his own interest.

Every man must know the following points around the machine gun emplacement:—houses, important dug-outs—*e.g.*, battalion and regimental command posts, the names of ruins, what is in them, if he has to cover any batteries with his fire in case of necessity, and if so, which; on what roads he must keep a special watch; how our own line runs generally, in order that he may recognise the danger zone quickly from the direction in which the light signals are being sent up.

Every man must be able to take a line across country to his emplacement, so that he is not bound to keep to roads and communication trenches, and so on. To guide him, he should make note of landmarks, such as prominent groups of trees, ruins, light-coloured fields, etc.

The main position to hold will always be the concrete emplacement. If the gun team takes up an alternative position, it will take with it 1,500 rounds, and water and cleaning material. Alarm practices should be arranged daily by the Gun Captain, including practice at the alternative positions.

Even under the heaviest fire, a sentry must be posted within calling or signalling distance. This sentry will only return to the gun when it has opened fire. The Gun Captain will arrange for his relief.

Every Gun Captain and man of the gun team must act deliberately, and not open fire before he really sees the enemy. Ammunition is costly, and can only be replaced with very great difficulty. The supply of ammunition takes precedence of the supply of rations.

The following points must be carefully considered by each man: From which direction can Tanks approach? Think out which roads and which dry, open fields are possible. Where can they be checked or stopped? How are they to be engaged? (a) By the construction of wire entanglements; at swampy or broad trenches; or at steep banks; (b) Employ armour-piercing ammunition, which is packed in separate boxes with red stripes down the sides. Aim low on the side, or—if using a telescope sight—aim at the loop holes.

Shoot at aircraft flying below 1,000 metres, with armour-piercing ammunition, but do not fire alone; co-operate with guns on the flanks.

On the gas alarm being given, put on gas masks, cover the machine gun with the tent square; sentries will keep a sharp look-out; pass on the alarm by ringing bells and beating gongs, but do not first whistle and call out so as to give the alarm, because in that case the gas masks will not be put on quickly enough. Rub the grease off the gun when the gas has blown over.

The following stores ought to be kept at every gun emplacement:—Iron rations of bread, water (for drinking and for the machine gun;—the latter kept in buckets or other vessels), meat, methylated spirits, candles, matches, and at least thirty-five hand grenades; also a reserve of bandages.

Each man must know the following routes:—
1. To the nearest ammunition dump.
2. To the nearest ration dump.
3. To the regimental and battalion command posts; to the Regimental Machine Gun Officer, and to the Company Commander on duty.
4. To the nearest Platoon (*Zug*) Commander.
5. *To the nearest water point.*
6. To the nearest medical dug-out.

Indents for equipment and material are to be sent through the Platoon or Company Commander on duty. These officers should also authorise the opening of iron rations.

The Gun Captain is responsible for the completeness and good condition of all the stores in the emplacement. He will check the following:—

1. The setting of the recoil intensifier. (This should be soaked in petroleum for one hour daily).
2. The condition of the barrel (?) (*Laufgang*).
3. The fusee spring tension for locks A. and B.
4. The lock guides. Are the springs in order? Have the cartridge support springs (*Patronenstutzfedern*) sheared?
5. Is there oil in the container?
6. Is the lock firmly seated?
7. Is there water in the jacket?
8. Is the ammunition in order? Are the guides of the belts straight and the cartridges tight?
9. Is there sufficient cleaning material in hand for three days? (Requisitions for fresh supplies should be made in plenty of time).
10. Is the sling (?) (*Umgeschnalle*) properly adjusted?
11. Is the dug-out clean? Has the gun been cleaned daily even if it has not been fired?
12. About 50 rounds should be fired at the ground frequently.

On being relieved, the gun captain has to hand over his emplacement in the sense of these orders to his successor. He must also make him acquainted with every observation made, with a list of completed work, with new work to be undertaken, with reconnaissance reports and any advice which he has to offer. A relief, in which the outgoing team goes away contenting itself with saying "Good evening, *au revoir*," is a crime against the spirit of comradeship.

If the enemy has pushed forward so far that no hope is left of holding out, then the last hand grenade must be used for the destruction of the machine gun. After that, the gun team must take to their revolvers. It should be a point of honour with every man not to allow a machine gun to fall into the hands of the enemy.

Section B.—EQUIPMENT.

(71) MARKINGS ON GERMAN AIRCRAFT.

German military and naval aeroplanes bear black crosses, shaped like "Iron Crosses," on the planes, rudder, and on both sides of the fuselage; machine of Commanders of battle plane flights, and naval aeroplanes often carry, on the rear edge of the lower planes, long red pennants in addition.

Infantry aeroplanes carry, at the outer ends of the lower planes, long black, white and red pennants, and fly lower than other aeroplanes.

German airships carry the German war flag. In addition, on the side of the forward part of the envelope, they are marked with the lettering Z, LZ, L, SL, or PL (in the case of the Navy, with the Arabic number following), and at each end (in front and in rear) of the balancing planes (*Oberkante*), and on each side of the direction rudders (*Unterkante*), with conspicuous black crosses shaped like "Iron Crosses."

(72) NOTES ON THE GERMAN "EMERGENCY CARRIAGE" MOUNTING.†

When the emergency carriage is used, the guns cannot usually fire further than 200 to 300 metres. This carriage can, therefore, only be used in places (especially in the front line trenches) situated at that distance from the targets in view. In any positions further to the rear, and in any intermediate positions, the sledge-carriage must be used if the maximum range of the machine gun is to be employed.

Section C.—ORGANISATION.

(73) PERSONNEL OF GERMAN LIGHT MACHINE GUN DETACHMENTS.

The personnel attached to the light '08/15 machine guns are grouped together as a "Company Machine Gun Section" (Inf. M.G. Trupp).

It consists of—
> For each Company: An experienced N.C.O., called armament N.C.O.; an assistant armourer.
> For each light machine gun: An N.C.O. or *Gefreiter* (Lance-Corporal) in charge; four gunners.

This personnel belongs to the strength of the Company.

It should consist entirely of N.C.O.'s and men "who can be relied upon, whose courage has been proved, and who have been distinguished for individual initiative."

Machine gunners are armed with an automatic revolver; training with model '98 rifle is limited to individual musketry practice.

"For ordinary marches, machine guns and all material are carried on the Company machine gun wagon, which follows the Company on a march."

When machine guns are being moved for action, to approach the enemy, to change position, they and the material are either carried by the personnel, or if circumstances and tactics permit, on small handcarts provided by the administration of the services.

If they are carried by the men, the crew has the assistance of a carrying party taken for the time being from the Company.‡

They are distributed as follows :—

> (a) Crew.—
>> The gunner in charge carries the steam escape pipe.
>> Gunner No. 1 carries the water-receiver, 2 spare gun barrels.
>> Gunner No. 2 (marksman) carries the gun, the crutch, a box of ammunition, model 16 (*Alarm-Kasten*).
>> Gunner No. 3 carries the bag for the mounting, a spare fusee spring, and an extractor. He takes turns with No. 2 in carrying the gun.
>> Gunner No. 4 carries two boxes of ammunition, Model 15 (b).

---

‡ *Carrying parties are armed with rifles, and at stopping places are treated as an infantry group.*

(b) Carrying Parties.—
> The soldier in charge carries a water receiver.
> No. 1 carries a water receiver and a box of ammunition, model 15; each of the 6 other men carry two boxes of ammunition.
> The gunner in charge directs the fire. He observes the fire and corrects the aim.
> As a general rule, the aim is obtained by firing a few cartridges in single shots, and then traversing fire is begun. Gunner No. 2, the marksman, lays the gun and fires. He must observe and correct his fire himself, and keep under cover as much as possible.
> The marksman ought to be able to serve his gun single-handed.
> Gunners No. 3 and 4 feed the gun.

Section D.—GENERAL.

(74) GERMAN INSTRUCTIONS FOR ENGAGING LOW-FLYING AEROPLANES BY INFANTRY AND MACHINE GUNS.

(Document is undated, but was apparently issued in 1917).

Procedure :—
- (a).—(1) If the aeroplane is flying in a direct or approximately direct line towards the observer; or
- (2) Is flying nearly straight overhead, away from the observer;

Fire must be delivered by infantry and machine guns.

Aim will be taken straight at the aeroplane.

Machine guns will not open searching fire on an approaching aeroplane, but will do so (three graduations), when the aeroplane is flying away. If the aeroplane is not flying directly towards the observer, its line of flight should be traversed with fire to a width of 50 metres.

Sights should be set as follows:—

Height of aeroplane.	*Sighting if approaching.*	*Sighting if flying away.*
100-400 m.	between 1400-1700 m.	400 m.
400-700 m.	,, 1700-2000 m.	400 m.
700-1000 m.	,, 1900-2000 m.	400 m.

Aeroplanes flying at a height exceeding 1,000 metres should not be fired on.

Fire should be opened, if possible, when the aeroplane is 2,000 metres distant. Sights, once set, should not be changed unless the aviator varies the height at which he is flying. Variation of range does not entail a corresponding modification of the sighting.

(b) If the aeroplane is flying across the front or obliquely to a flank, it will be engaged by machine guns only.

All machine guns will open searching fire at such a distance in front of the aeroplane, that the latter must traverse the cone of fire. The allowances, given below, for aiming in front of the aeroplane must be made when opening fire. The process must be repeated as soon as the distance between the aiming point and the aeroplane has been reduced, either by one-half or to the amount laid down for the preceeding zone.‡

Orders must be given quickly and decisively by the Commander controlling the fire.

Fire should be delivered as follows:—

Range from 100-600 metres, sights set for 600 metres, searching fire (three graduations), aiming point five aeroplane lengths in front. Range from 600-1,000 metres, angle less than 45 degrees, sights set for 900 metres, searching fire (three graduations), aiming point eleven aeroplane lengths in front.

Range from 6,000-,1000 metres, angle exceeding 45 degrees, sights set for 650 metres, searching fire (three graduations), aiming point eleven aeroplane lengths in front.

Range from 1,000-1,300 metres, angle less than 45 degrees, sights set for 1,200 metres, searching fire (three graduations), aiming point sixteen aeroplane lengths in front.

Range from 1,000-1,300 metres, angle exceeding 45 degrees, sights set for 850 metres, searching fire (three graduations), aiming point sixteen aeroplane lengths.

The length of an aeroplane is taken as being about eight metres, and the velocity 160 km. per hour (100 m.p.h.).

(75) INFORMATION FROM A PRISONER OF THE 208TH GERMAN DIVISION.

In this Division, 80 men and 8 machine guns is the establishment of each Machine Gun Company; one Machine Gun Company is

---

‡ *Note.—The order apparently divides the ranges into three " Zones," viz :—*
   100-600 metres.
   600-1,000   ,,
   1,000-1,300   ,,

attached to each Battalion, making a total of 24 guns in the Regiment. No other Machine Gun units are attached.

On coming into the line, each gun brought up 2,000 rounds of ammunition, but, 11,000 rounds were found in the position occupied. This includes armour piercing ("K"), but prisoner was unable to give the percentage. "K" ammunition is mostly used against aircraft. Each gun in line has a crew of 6 men, and 3 or 4 men when in reserve.

In trench warfare, probably only 2 machine guns per Battalion would actually be in front trenches, the remainder being distributed between the support and reserve lines.

The emplacements in the front line are, when possible, built about 1 yard in front of the actual line, so as to enable them to enfilade the front of the trench. In a hurriedly-constructed line this is not always possible, and as no dug-outs being available, guns are kept in the bottom of the trench. When warned by the sentries that our barrage had lifted, the guns are immediately placed on the parapet.

Every gun usually had an alternative emplacement 10 yards right or left. These emplacements were sighted by the Section Commander.

Prisoner stated that they never pushed their guns forward into shell holes, as their Regimental Commander did not approve of it, and stated that marksmen sections only should be sent to occupy these positions. Reserve emplacements are very often organized in shell holes, in which case he considered the usual method adopted is as shown below. These emplacements are not occupied when an attack is expected, the guns having been withdrawn to a protected spot.

The machine guns in reserve rarely fired through our barrage, for they were afraid of firing on their own men. He had no idea as to what distance in front we put our barrage when consolidating a trench.

If forced to retire, the guns are taken right back and the reserve guns come into action. According to the situation the guns are then brought up again from the rear to reinforce, or take up a new position. Machine gunners are also ready to be brought up in cars in the event of a successful attack by us.

When possible, the usual method adopted is for pairs of guns to form a barrage, with a single gun to cover the intervening ground, as shown below—

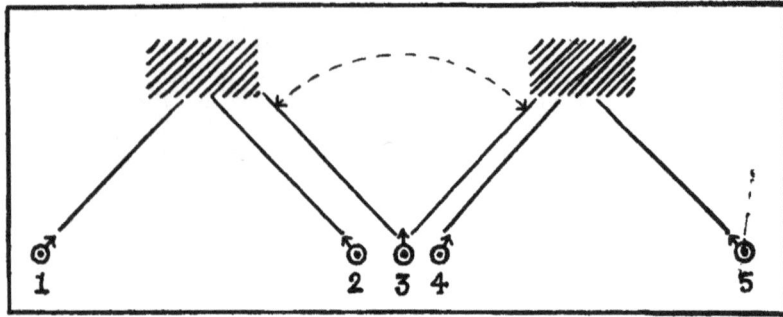

Figure 7.

i.e., 1 and 2, 4 and 5, form a barrage and 3 covers the intervening space between these pairs of guns.

RELIEFS.—Reliefs are nearly always carried out across country, except when no firing is going on. Villages within range are always avoided. A large number of casualties are caused to stretcher bearers on the roads as they are unable to go across country.

CONFIDENTIAL.

40/W.O./4331

FOR OFFICIAL USE ONLY.

SUMMARY OF MACHINE GUN INTELLIGENCE

No. 3.

Issued by the General Staff.

JULY, 1917.

PRINTED AT THE MACHINE GUN SCHOOL, MACHINE GUN TRAINING CENTRE.
UNDER THE AUTHORITY OF HIS MAJESTY'S STATIONERY OFFICE,

CONTENTS.

Part I. Training.

Section *a.* Personnel.
,, *b.* Transport.
,, *c.* Co-operation.
,, *d.* Gas.
,, *e.* Operations—Notes on.
,, *f.* General.

Part II. Technical.

Section *a.* Equipment.
,, *b.* Demonstrations.
,, *c.* Experiments.
,, *d.* Tests.
,, *e.* General.

Part III.
Machine Gun Intelligence of Foreign Countries.

Section *a.* Tactics.
,, *b.* Equipment.
,, *c.* Organization.
,, *d.* General.

NOTE.—With the exception of those paragraphs marked with an asterisk, the information contained in this summary has been extracted from reports received from General Headquarters of Expeditionary Forces.

PART I.—TRAINING.

Section A.—PERSONNEL.

(54) Owing to the increased use of machine guns for indirect fire and, particularly, for barrage fire, a higher standard of training is required for all ranks in :—

    (i.) Rapid laying out of aiming posts for indirect fire.

    (ii.) Firing by the watch with a time table of "Lifts."

In connection with this a barrage drill, embodying the principal points for carrying out preliminary training for barrage fire, is under consideration.

During the training of Officers, special attention should be paid to the following :—

    (i.) Appreciation of ground.

    (ii.) Tactical schemes including barrage fire.

    (iii.) Finding position by resection.

In some units N.C.O.'s have received a special course of instruction in map reading and indirect fire, with the object of enabling them to supervise firing from time tables should the Officer in charge become a casualty.

Where other facilities do not exist, practice with ball ammunition, on the 25 yards range, can be carried out for training personnel in firing to a given time-table, laying out zero lines, "lifts," concentrations, etc.

Section B.—TRANSPORT.

See under Part II, Section (c). Experiments.

Section C.—CO-OPERATION.

(55) With Lewis Guns.

Reports on recent operations again seem to show that more co-operation between the Vickers and Lewis guns might have existed. In every area there are certain localities where the field of fire is so limited that, whereas efficient use of the sustained fire power of a Vickers gun could not be made, the short but rapid bursts of fire from the Lewis gun would cover the ground adequately.

Reports go on to state that, during the period of taking up the occupation on the definite line of defence, the necessity for co-operation is specially apparent. Without this, guns of one class will be moved without any thought of the other, whereas they should combine to create the strongest possible defence.

(56) Co-operation with Infantry.

A report on a machine gun barrage states that, immediately the S.O.S. signal went up, all machine guns opened fire. On both occasions when this signal was received, each gun had fired at least 100 rounds before the artillery barrage opened. The report continues: "The infantry of the battalions are beginning to lose their fear of our own machine guns, and to place more confidence in the machine gun barrage than they did formerly. If it was explained to the infantry how and where machine guns were fired, their confidence would be increased still further, and the moral effect of the support rendered by machine gun fire would be greatly enhanced."

(57) Co-operation with Anti-Aircraft Batteries.

Possible co-operation between machine guns specially detached for engaging low flying hostile aircraft, and neighbouring anti-aircraft batteries must not be overlooked.

In certain cases an observer from an anti-aircraft battery was posted with the machine gun detachment in a forward area. This observer was in direct communication with his battery and acted as a F.O.O. His duty was to give early warning of the approach of low flying hostile aircraft which could not be observed from the anti-aircraft battery positions.

This is very important: as a general rule, the anti-aircraft observers are too far back and out of touch with the troops holding the line.

Section D.—GAS.

NIL.

Section E.—OPERATIONS.

(58) ARRANGEMENTS FOR BARRAGE FIRE.

The value of an organized system of machine gun fire, both in attack and defence, is shown by the following report on the machine gun barrage during a certain operation.

(i.) The frontage dealt with was 2,000 yards.

(ii.) The number of guns available was 23. On that account, each group of guns had, approximately, twice as much ground to deal with as it ought to have had. But on the frontage there were certain localities which were known to be dangerous, and these were selected for special treatment, and concentration of fire. The selection of these localities was afterwards found to be justified by the reports of prisoners as to lines of approach, assembly and concentration movements of the enemy.

(iii.) All groups were in direct communication with their respective Company Headquarters by telephone, and any information, received from Brigade and Artillery liaison Officers as to impending attacks, concentration of the enemy, etc., was quickly transmitted to the Officers in charge of groups. No complaints were received from the infantry as to clearances, and all theory was justified in practice.

(iv.) The average expenditure of ammunition from zero to zero plus 48 hours, was 12,000 rounds per gun. All barrels were new at the commencement of operations but, after 48 hours firing, it was found necessary to renew most of them, especially those firing directly over the heads of our infantry.

(v.) Several prisoners were interrogated as to the effect of the fire. They were all of the opinion that many of their casualties were due to machine gun fire.

NOTES.—Two rates of fire were employed in this operation.

(i.) *Intense Fire.*—One belt per gun every two minutes. S.O.S. fire was always to be intense fire.

(ii.) *Searching Fire.*—One belt per gun every 15 minutes.

The following special instructions were issued to Officers in charge of groups :—

- (i.) The defensive barrage will be brought down on the S.O.S. lines immediately the S.O.S. signal is fired.
- (ii.) Search all places where the enemy is likely to assemble.
- (iii.) Search all dangerous localities.
- (iv.) Be prepared to deal with counter-attacks at any moment.
- (v.) Officers in charge of groups must keep in touch with the situation.

At zero hour each gun had 6,000 rounds of S.A.A. alongside its position for re-filling purposes.

(59) ACTION AT GREENLAND HILL.

During the recent attack on GREENLAND HILL, machine guns were employed to place a protective barrage across the front of the captured position, in case of enemy counter-attack. From ZERO plus 1 to ZERO plus 18 minutes, the guns allotted for barrage fire had orders to engage certain objectives, (——— WOOD, CARROT TRENCH, CYPRUS TRENCH, and CHALK PIT). After carrying out these tasks, they were then laid on the barrage lines.

No serious enemy counter-attack developed until 10 p.m. on the night after the position was captured. On the evidence of our own troops in the front line, the machine gun barrage was put down with such speed and accuracy, "that the enemy failed to get further than his own parapet."

Two more counter-attacks, at 12-30 a.m. and 3-30 a.m., were dealt with in a similar manner.

This brings out the great value of the machine gun barrage during the small interval of time that usually elapses between the S.O.S. signal and the full artillery barrage. If the machine gun barrage can go down during that interval, and there is no reason why it should not, the chances of successful hostile counter-attack are greatly reduced. If the machine guns had waited for the artillery barrage before opening fire, this effect would have been lost. This emphasizes the necessity for S.O.S. observation either from the actual gun position or, if that is not possible, from some forward observation post in communication with the guns.

(60) AIRCRAFT AND CONCEALMENT OF GUNS.

Reports tend to confirm that the enemy is making special endeavours to locate the exact positions of machine guns employed for barrage work. The procedure is nearly always the same ; early in the morning following the first protective barrage, a hostile aeroplane flies at low altitude over the vicinity of the guns, until it has succeeded in locating them. The increase in the quantity, weight and accuracy of subsequent shell fire on those particular guns, has been noted afterwards in every case.

In the operations quoted in paragraph 7, an aeroplane came over the day after the assault, and obviously succeeded in locating some of the guns in a certain trench, as the subsequent shelling showed. Three guns were put out of action, but the trench did not receive the attention it would have done if all the guns had been suspected or located.

Another report states :—" The enemy appears to make great efforts to locate and silence these (barrage) machine guns, even using aeroplanes and dropping lights over the gun positions. When located, a heavy barrage of 5.9 in. shells usually follows."

The importance of taking the greatest care in the concealment of machine guns for barrage fire from aerial observation—both by naked eye and by camera—is therefore emphasised.

If there is any reason to suspect that the position has been located by the enemy, the guns should, if possible, move to a new position from which to carry out their tasks, so as to escape the shelling which will inevitably follow.

In certain cases machine guns have been detailed for the special purpose of engaging hostile aircraft from carefully selected forward positions. Being detached from the main group, these guns would not draw fire upon the batteries, even though the enemy spotted and shelled those anti-aircraft machine guns themselves. They should of course have alternative positions handy.

(61) ADVANCED POSTS, STRONG POINTS, ETC., are better defended by machine guns placed *outside* and *to flanks*, rather than in the locality itself. To have such a position bristling with machine guns does not necessarily indicate strength ; it may mean weakness, especially if the position is heavily shelled with the resulting casualties in men and material.

(62) MACHINE GUN SCREEN FOR OUTPOSTS, ETC.

In some notes on some recent semi-open fighting, the value of machine gun fire as a screen for outposts and patrols is pointed out. A machine gun barrage placed on an enemy front line was found by one Infantry Brigade to lessen considerably the risk of detection by hostile observers. Also it attracts less attention than an artillery barrage.

The arrangements for covering fire of this nature, especially when used in connection with patrols and small offensive units, must be laid down definitely beforehand.

Section F.—GENERAL.

(63) CONTROL OF INDIRECT FIRE.

On several occasions long range fire by several groups of machine guns has been successfully directed from forward observation posts. Control was maintained by flash signals, arranged in a special code, and by telephone. Many parties of the enemy were scattered and casualties inflicted.

(64) STOPPAGES DUE TO BRICK DUST.

During the recent fighting in the housed area west of LENS, instances occurred of machine guns being clogged by the very fine brick dust raised by the bombardment. One of the guns had to be stripped owing to a stoppage; the dust settled on it to such an extent that, though the stoppage was corrected, the gun was in a worse condition for firing than before. The brick dust, mixing with the oil, made a sticky paste very hard to wipe off, and it was found necessary to wash several guns in water to do away with it.

The dust also penetrated the wooden belt boxes and made the belts unfit for use; the ammunition in the steel boxes remained clean.

Under similar circumstances, care should be taken to keep all ammunition boxes tightly closed; wooden boxes should, if possible, be kept wrapped up until they are required for firing.

(65) CONCEALMENT OF GUNS.

During a recent action, the following system was adopted by certain groups of machine guns used for barrage fire, for concealing the positions of the guns.

The tripods were mounted as low as possible in the parapet or shell hole; they were then buried in earth, etc., until only the working parts were clear. The gun was then mounted, firing flush with the level of the parapet, or lip of the shell hole. Over the gun was then put a small, light wooden frame, camouflaged with sandbags and earth to match the nature of the immediate surroundings, concealing the gun both from the front and from above. It was also arranged that the gun could fire without this camouflage being removed.

All ammunition boxes were placed in recesses, so that to the hostile aeroplane, though the trench looked occupied, neither guns nor stores were visible to indicate the possible presence of machine guns. The report states that this system proved effective.

PART II.—TECHNICAL.

Section A.—EQUIPMENT.

(66) SUPPLY OF SPARE PARTS.

It should be realised that in an operation of any magnitude the wear and tear of spare parts and barrels is bound to be above the normal. With a view to helping the service concerned in making adequate preparations, a forecast of material required should always be made well in advance.

(67) YUKON PACK.

Although these carriers were used under the worst conditions during the fighting on VIMY RIDGE, they were most successful and enabled the men to carry bigger loads than would have been possible otherwise.

*Suggested methods of carrying machine gun equipment are shown in the figures.

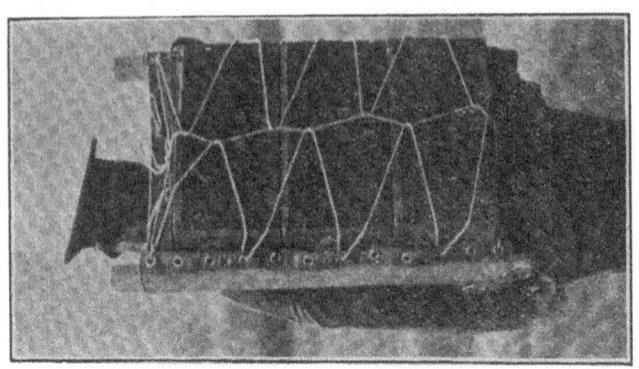
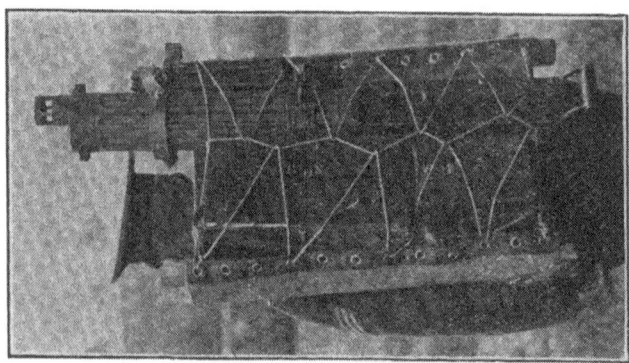

FIGURE 8,

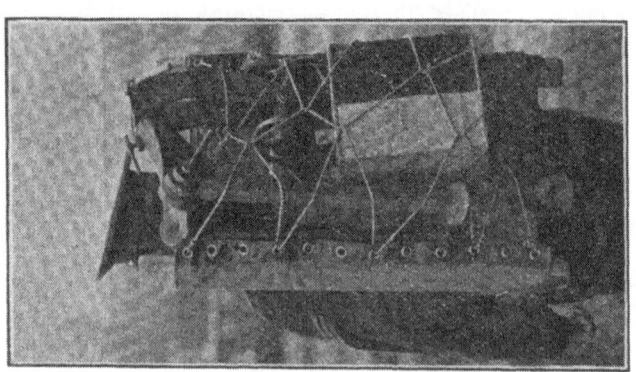

Note that the cross lacing is looped in the centre, over a cord which runs from the bottom to the top of the pack and is fastened at the top by a slip knot. By slipping this knot and pulling out the centre cord, the whole lacing will fall apart thus enabling the load to be removed in a few seconds.

(68) AMMUNITION BELTS.

Reports show that many stoppages have been caused by belts not having been kept clean and dry. Every effort should be made to do this. A sandbag or waterproof sheet should be placed on wet and muddy ground to receive empty belts.

During the recent fighting on VIMY RIDGE, tarpaulins measuring 10' × 15' were used by several machine gun batteries to make temporary rainproof shelters for the belt loaders. This is stated to have been of great value during the heavy snowstorms of the 9th and 10th April.

(69) CARRYING BELT BOXES.

Several reports state that an effective belt box carrier can be extemporised by connecting the handles of two boxes by two straps, one for each shoulder, and each about one foot long. These are then slung over the shoulders, one box on the back and the other on the chest, thus leaving the hands free. In some cases quick release devices have been added to the ends of the connecting straps, thus enabling the two boxes to be disconnected quickly, while the shoulder straps can be retained by the wearer. The salvage dumps can often supply coat straps off webbing equipment, which answer the purpose very well.

(70) MUZZLE CUP MARK II., SCREWED PATTERN.

All reports continue to state that these are very satisfactory. In one or two instances it is said that difficulty has been experienced in removing them after much firing. If the threads on the cup and the barrel are cleaned and slightly oiled before screwing up, this difficulty should not occur, and according to the majority of reports, has not occurred.

(71) NEW BARRELS.

In a few cases, new barrels are reported to have been slightly over length, thus causing a No. 3 stoppage, due to the extractor being prevented from rising. This can be remedied by the artificer filing away a portion of the barrel block near the extractor way, top and bottom.

Section B.—DEMONSTRATIONS.
NIL.
Section C.—EXPERIMENTS.

(72) COMPASS TÓWER.*

Further experiments have been made with this device at the Machine Gun Training Centre, and details are circulated for information of a modified form of tower made of mahogany, which can be easily made in a workshop.

Figures 9 and 10 show the construction and dimensions of this model. The fitting is clamped on to the crosshead joint pin by the butterfly nut A. The compass itself is secured by tightening the screw B, thus clamping the compass case firmly against the two screw heads C C. This form of fastening will take different sizes of compass case.

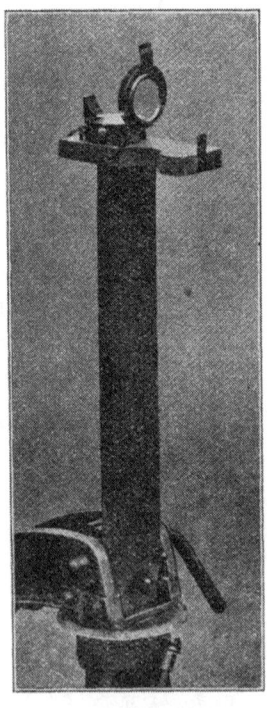

FIGURE 9.

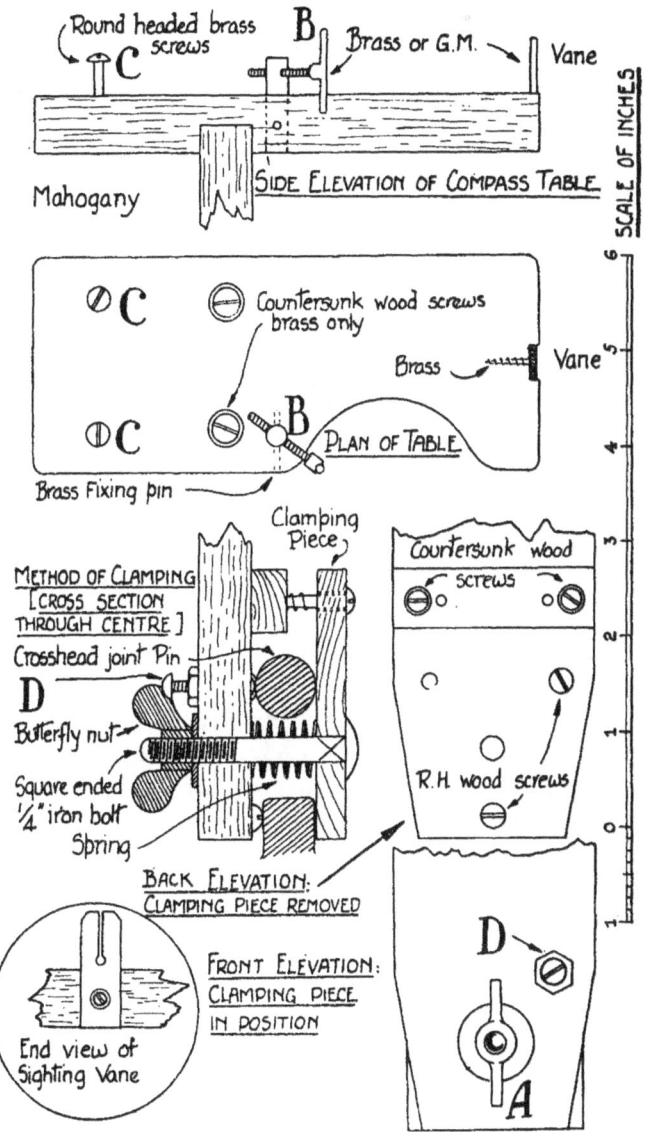

Figure 10.

After the tower has been fixed into position, the compass should be adjusted so that the lubber line passes through the sighting vane.

To check that the line of sight from the compass will be parallel to the axis of the bore, the following simple method can be employed:—

- (i.) Mount the gun on the tripod, select any aiming mark, and lay the gun upon it.
- (ii.) Taking care not to move the tripod or crosshead, remove the gun and fix the compass tower and compass in position.
- (iii.) Adjust the compass so that the lubber line passes through the sight vane. When this is done, if the line of sight through the compass is now accurately on the aiming mark, no further adjustment is required.
- (iv.) If the line of sight is not on the aiming mark, it can be brought on to it by adjustment of the small screw D, which rotates the tower sufficiently for the purpose. When the final adjustment has been made, the lock nut on the screw D should be tightened up to prevent this screw working loose.

Section D.—TESTS.

NIL.

Section E.—GENERAL.

(73) METHOD OF LAYING A GUN ON A GIVEN COMPASS BEARING.

The following method of laying a gun on a given bearing has been reported to be simple and effective.

The Officer or N.C.O. goes out about 20 yards in the approximate direction in which the gun has to fire. He then takes a bearing on to the gun with the prismatic compass: at the same time, the gun is laid on the compass and the reading on the direction dial noted. The compass reading—which is really the back bearing of the compass position from the gun—is converted into a forward bearing by subtracting $180°$ from it.

The difference between this forward bearing and the bearing on which the gun has to be laid, is then added to, or subtracted from the reading already noted on the direction dial, No. 1 tapping the gun right or left as may be necessary. The gun will then be laid on the required bearing, and an auxiliary aiming mark aligned in the usual manner.

Part III.—Machine Gun Intelligence of Foreign Countries.

Section A.—TACTICS.

(74) HEAVY MACHINE GUN EMPLACEMENTS.

A captured German gunner stated that owing to the insufficiency of artillery ammunition, more and more reliance would have to be placed on heavy machine gun emplacements which the enemy is constructing at irregular intervals over the back area.

(75) LESSONS LEARNT FROM FIGHTING ON THE AISNE.
(Translated from a German Document.)

Machine guns should only exceptionally be posted in the front line. On principle, emplacements should be inconspicuous, and tunnels (including the entrances), well camouflaged. There should be no machine gun nests, for the latter will be detected by aeroplanes, and destroyed by the artillery. No firing should take place from these emplacements before the infantry attack. The employment of massed Machine Gun Companies is to be recommended. Zones of machine guns should be formed between the second and third lines, the guns being sited according to the field of fire obtainable. These zones of machine guns should be reinforced by light Minenwerfer and Granatenwerfer. The supply of ammunition in belts should be ample, at least 4,000 rounds per gun.

(76) FRENCH TACTICS IN THE DEFENCE OF WOODS.
(Translation of a German Document.)

The French practice is to bring up small posts and machine guns to the edge of the wood, which they surround with barbed wire entanglements. They build up defence works inside the wood, consisting of low blockhouses, connected by an entanglement. Obstacles are placed from the fringe of the wood to the centre in such a way as to lead the enemy into blind alleys, which are exposed to machine gun fire. Snipers and machine guns in the trees keep the tracks under their fire. Great use is made of sound signals, which are intended to warn the defenders, in time, of the enemy's approach. (In the Vosges the "Chasseurs Alpins" hid in the trees and gave the alarm to the garrison by imitating the cries of birds.) The defence is of an offensive nature (prepared ambuscades), and every attempt is made to fall on the flank of the enemy who is advancing unmethodically.

Snipers or machine guns hidden in trees must be watched. Before bringing in the main body of assault troops these marksmen must be rendered harmless by directing machine gun fire on the tops of the trees.

Woods afford very good cover for the establishment of surprise works, such as machine gun blockhouses.

Section B.—EQUIPMENT.

(77) GERMAN LIGHT MACHINE GUNS IN REGIMENTS.

Prisoners of the 46th I.R. stated that their regiment had three Machine Gun Companies, each armed with 9 guns; three of these were issued to each Machine Gun Company on arrival at the Western Front. In addition the regiment received 45 light machine guns on the 13th June. This represents a complete issue of the new light machine gun.

(78) GERMAN AMMUNITION :

(Translation of a German Document).

The employment of "S" (iron cartridge case) ammunition, in machine guns, has brought to light instances of cases splitting and fouling the mechanism during continuous fire. Experiments with a view to obtaining an iron case equally suitable for rifle and machine gun (Dinheitshulse) are being continued. Meanwhile, "S" ammunition with brass cases is being supplied for machine guns and anti-aircraft defence in Germany.

Section C.—ORGANISATION.

NIL.

Section D.—GENERAL.

NIL.

www.ingramcontent.com/pod-product-compliance
Lightning Source LLC
Chambersburg PA
CBHW051713040426
42446CB00008B/854